822.33 Shakespeare
W 7   The l... Y0-CVJ-955
Yale   Henry the Eighth.

DATE DUE

10/23/14			

WITHDRAWN

THE YALE SHAKESPEARE

Edited by

Wilbur L. Cross   Tucker Brooke

Published under the Direction
of the
Department of English, Yale University,
on the Fund
Given to the Yale University Press in 1917
by the Members of the
Kingsley Trust Association
(Scroll and Key Society of Yale College)
To Commemorate the Seventy-Fifth Anniversary
of the Founding of the Society

·: *The Yale Shakespeare* :·

THE LIFE OF KING HENRY THE EIGHTH

EDITED BY

JOHN M. BERDAN

AND

TUCKER BROOKE

NEW HAVEN · YALE UNIVERSITY PRESS

COPYRIGHT, 1925
BY YALE UNIVERSITY PRESS

First published, September, 1925
Second printing, October, 1959

Printed in the United States of America

CONTENTS

		Page
The Text	. . . . . .	1
Notes	. . . .	119
Appendix A.	Sources of the Play . .	147
Appendix B.	The History of the Play .	150
Appendix C.	Authorship of the Play .	155
Appendix D.	The Text of the Present Edition	159
Appendix E.	Suggestions for Collateral Reading . . .	161
Index of Words Glossed		163

This facsimile reproduces an engraved portrait of King Henry VIII in the Elizabethan Club. It represents the king as he appeared in 1544, near the end of his life. The engraving illustrates the earliest period of the art in England and was executed by Cornelius Metzys (1511?-1550?), son of the Flemish painter Quentin Metzys.

[DRAMATIS PERSONÆ.

KING HENRY THE EIGHTH.
CARDINAL WOLSEY.
CARDINAL CAMPEIUS.
CAPUCIUS, *Ambassador from the Emperor Charles V.*
CRANMER, *Archbishop of Canterbury.*
DUKE OF NORFOLK.
DUKE OF SUFFOLK.
DUKE OF BUCKINGHAM.
EARL OF SURREY.
LORD CHANCELLOR.
LORD CHAMBERLAIN.
GARDINER, *Bishop of Winchester.*
BISHOP OF LINCOLN.
LORD ABERGAVENNY.
LORD SANDYS.
SIR THOMAS LOVELL.
SIR HENRY GUILFORD.
SIR ANTHONY DENNY.
SIR NICHOLAS VAUX.
CROMWELL, *Servant to Wolsey.*
GRIFFITH, *Gentleman-Usher to Queen Katharine.*
DOCTOR BUTTS, *Physician to the King.*
BRANDON, and a Sergeant-at-Arms.

QUEEN KATHARINE, *Wife to King Henry.*
ANNE BULLEN, *her Maid of Honour; later Queen.*
An Old Lady, *Friend to Anne Bullen.*
PATIENCE, *Woman to Queen Katharine.*

Secretaries to Wolsey; Three Gentlemen; Garter King-at-Arms; Surveyor to the Duke of Buckingham; Door-keeper of the Council Chamber; Porter, and his Man; Page to Gardiner; A Crier; Several Lords and Ladies in the Dumb Shows; Women attending upon the Queen; Spirits which appear to her; Scribes, Officers, Guards, etc.

SCENE: *London and Westminster; once at Kimbolton.*]

The Famous History of the Life of King Henry the Eighth

The Prologue

I come no more to make you laugh: things now,
That bear a weighty and a serious brow,
Sad, high, and working, full of state and woe,
Such noble scenes as draw the eye to flow,   4
We now present. Those that can pity here
May, if they think it well, let fall a tear;
The subject will deserve it. Such as give
Their money out of hope they may believe,   8
May here find truth too. Those that come to see
Only a show or two, and so agree
The play may pass, if they be still and willing,
I'll undertake may see away their shilling   12
Richly in two short hours. Only they
That come to hear a merry, bawdy play,
A noise of targets, or to see a fellow
In a long motley coat guarded with yellow,   16
Will be deceiv'd; for, gentle hearers, know,
To rank our chosen truth with such a show
As fool and fight is, besides forfeiting
Our own brains, and the opinion that we bring,   20
To make that only true we now intend,
Will leave us never an understanding friend.
Therefore, for goodness' sake, and as you are known
The first and happiest hearers of the town,   24

The Prologue; *cf. n.*
3 Sad: *serious*   working: *full of pathos*   state: *dignity*
9 truth; *cf. n.*   12 shilling; *cf. n.*
16 In . . . coat; *cf. n.*   guarded: *trimmed*
19 As fool and fight is; *cf. n.*   20 opinion: *reputation, intention*
21 intend: *undertake*   22 Will leave us: *cf. n.*

Be sad, as we would make ye: think ye see
The very persons of our noble story
As they were living; think you see them great,
And follow'd with the general throng and sweat   28
Of thousand friends; then in a moment see
How soon this mightiness meets misery:
And if you can be merry then, I'll say
A man may weep upon his wedding day.   32

ACT FIRST

Scene One

[London. An Antechamber in the Palace]

Enter the Duke of Norfolk at one door; at the other, the Duke of Buckingham and the Lord Abergavenny.

  Buck. Good morrow, and well met. How have you done,
Since last we saw in France?
  Nor.   I thank your Grace,
Healthful; and ever since a fresh admirer
Of what I saw there.
  Buck.   An untimely ague   4
Stay'd me a prisoner in my chamber, when
Those suns of glory, those two lights of men,
Met in the vale of Andren.
  Nor.   'Twixt Guynes and Arde:
I was then present, saw them salute on horseback;   8
Beheld them, when they lighted, how they clung
In their embracement, as they grew together;

25, 26 *Cf. n.*
Scene One S. d. Duke of Norfolk, Duke of Buckingham, Lord
    Abergavenny; *cf. n.*   2 saw: *met*
6 Those suns of glory; *cf. n.*   7 vale of Andren; *cf. n.*

King Henry the Eighth, I. i.

Which had they, what four thron'd ones could have weigh'd
Such a compounded one?
Buck. All the whole time 12
I was my chamber's prisoner.
Nor. Then you lost
The view of earthly glory: men might say,
Till this time pomp was single, but now married
To one above itself. Each following day 16
Became the next day's master, till the last
Made former wonders its. To-day the French
All clinquant, all in gold, like heathen gods,
Shone down the English; and to-morrow they 20
Made Britain India: every man that stood
Show'd like a mine. Their dwarfish pages were
As cherubins, all gilt: the madams, too,
Not us'd to toil, did almost sweat to bear 24
The pride upon them, that their very labour
Was to them as a painting. Now this masque
Was cried incomparable; and the ensuing night
Made it a fool and beggar. The two kings, 28
Equal in lustre, were now best, now worst,
As presence did present them; him in eye
Still him in praise; and, being present both,
'Twas said they saw but one; and no discerner 32
Durst wag his tongue in censure. When these suns—
For so they phrase 'em—by their heralds challeng'd
The noble spirits to arms, they did perform
Beyond thought's compass; that former fabulous story, 36
Being now seen possible enough, got credit,
That Bevis was believ'd.

12 All the whole time; *cf. n.* 18 its; *cf. n.*
19 clinquant: *glittering* 30 him in eye: *the one present*
38 That: *so that* Bevis; *cf. n.*

Buck.   O, you go far!
Nor. As I belong to worship, and affect
In honour honesty, the tract of everything   40
Would by a good discourser lose some life,
Which action's self was tongue to.
Buck.   All was royal;
To the disposing of it nought rebell'd,
Order gave each thing view; the office did   44
Distinctly his full function. Who did guide,
I mean, who set the body and the limbs
Of this great sport together?
Nor.   As you guess.
One certes, that promises no element   48
In such a business.
Buck.   I pray you, who, my lord?
Nor. All this was order'd by the good discretion
Of the right reverend Cardinal of York.
Buck. The devil speed him! no man's pie is freed   52
From his ambitious finger. What had he
To do in these fierce vanities? I wonder
That such a keech can with his very bulk
Take up the rays o' the beneficial sun,   56
And keep it from the earth.
Nor.   Surely, sir,
There's in him stuff that puts him to these ends;
For, being not propp'd by ancestry, whose grace
Chalks successors their way, nor call'd upon   60
For high feats done to the crown; neither allied
To eminent assistants; but, spider-like,
Out of his self-drawing web, a' gives us note,
The force of his own merit makes his way;   64

39 worship: *noble rank*   40 tract: *course*
41, 42 Would . . . tongue to: *could not be presented even by a skilful narrator with the vividness which the reality expressed*
42-47 *Cf. n.*   54 fierce: *extravagant*
55 keech: *lump of fat*   63 Out . . . web; *cf. n.*   a': *he*

King Henry the Eighth, I. i.

A gift that heaven gives for him, which buys
A place next to the king.
 Aber.   I cannot tell
What heaven hath given him: let some graver eye
Pierce into that; but I can see his pride   68
Peep through each part of him: whence has he that?
If not from hell, the devil is a niggard,
Or has given all before, and he begins
A new hell in himself.
 Buck.   Why the devil,   72
Upon this French going-out, took he upon him,
Without the privity o' the king, to appoint
Who should attend on him? He makes up the file
Of all the gentry; for the most part such   76
To whom as great a charge as little honour
He meant to lay upon,—and his own letter
(The honourable board of council out)
Must fetch him in,—he papers.
 Aber.   I do know   80
Kinsmen of mine, three at the least, that have
By this so sicken'd their estates, that never
They shall abound as formerly.
 Buck.   O, many
Have broke their backs with laying manors on 'em   84
For this great journey. What did this vanity
But minister communication of
A most poor issue?
 Nor.   Grievingly I think,
The peace between the French and us not values   88
The cost that did conclude it.
 Buck.   Every man,

---

74 privi y: *knowledge*   76-80 *Cf. n.*
80 fetch him in: *cheat*   papers: *lists*
84 with . . . on 'em: *by selling manorial estates in order to buy personal equipment*   86 minister communication; *cf. n*

After the hideous storm that follow'd, was
A thing inspir'd; and, not consulting, broke
Into a general prophecy: That this tempest, 92
Dashing the garment of this peace, aboded
The sudden breach on 't.
　　Nor.　　　　　　　　Which is budded out;
For France hath flaw'd the league, and hath attach'd
Our merchants' goods at Bordeaux.
　　Aber.　　　　　　　　　　Is it therefore 96
Th' ambassador is silenc'd?
　　Nor.　　　　　　　　Marry, is 't.
　　Aber. A proper title of a peace; and purchas'd
At a superfluous rate!
　　Buck.　　　　　　　Why, all this business
Our reverend cardinal carried.
　　Nor.　　　　　　　　Like it your Grace, 100
The state takes notice of the private difference
Betwixt you and the cardinal. I advise you,—
And take it from a heart that wishes towards you
Honour and plenteous safety,—that you read　　104
The cardinal's malice and his potency
Together; to consider further that
What his high hatred would effect wants not
A minister in his power. You know his nature, 108
That he's revengeful; and I know his sword
Hath a sharp edge: it's long, and 't may be said,
It reaches far; and where 'twill not extend,
Thither he darts it. Bosom up my counsel, 112
You'll find it wholesome. Lo where comes that rock
That I advise your shunning.

90 hideous storm; *cf. n.*　　　　　95 For . . . league; *cf. n.*
97 Th' ambassador is silenc'd; *cf. n.*
100 Like . . . Grace: *may it please your Grace*

King Henry the Eighth, I. i.

Enter Cardinal Wolsey,—the Purse borne before him, —certain of the Guard, and two Secretaries with papers. The Cardinal in his passage fixeth his eye on Buckingham, and Buckingham on him, both full of disdain.

Car. The Duke of Buckingham's surveyor, ha?
Where's his examination?
 Secr.   Here, so please you.   116
 Car. Is he in person ready?
 Secr.   Ay, please your Grace.
 Car. Well, we shall then know more; and Buckingham
Shall lessen this big look.
     [Exeunt Cardinal and his Train.]
 Buck. This butcher's cur is venom'd-mouth'd, and I   120
Have not the power to muzzle him; therefore best
Not wake him in his slumber. A beggar's book
Outworths a noble's blood.
 Nor.   What! are you chaf'd?
Ask God for temperance; that's th' appliance only   124
Which your disease requires.
 Buck.   I read in's looks
Matter against me; and his eye revil'd
Me as his abject object: at this instant
He bores me with some trick. He's gone to the king: 128
I'll follow, and outstare him.
 Nor.   Stay, my lord,
And let your reason with your choler question
What 'tis you go about. To climb steep hills

---

115 *Cf. n.*   120 This butcher's cur; *cf. n.*   venom'd: *venomous*
122 book: *learning*
124 temperance: *moderation*   appliance: *remedy*
127 abject object: *object of his contempt*   128 bores: *cheats*

Requires slow pace at first: anger is like 132
A full hot horse, who being allow'd his way,
Self-mettle tires him. Not a man in England
Can advise me like you: be to yourself
As you would to your friend.
  Buck.   I'll to the king; 136
And from a mouth of honour quite cry down
This Ipswich fellow's insolence, or proclaim
There's difference in no persons.
  Nor.   Be advis'd;
Heat not a furnace for your foe so hot 140
That it do singe yourself. We may outrun
By violent swiftness that which we run at,
And lose by overrunning. Know you not,
The fire that mounts the liquor till 't run o'er, 144
In seeming to augment it wastes it? Be advis'd:
I say again, there is no English soul
More stronger to direct you than yourself,
If with the sap of reason you would quench, 148
Or but allay, the fire of passion.
  Buck.   Sir,
I am thankful to you, and I'll go along
By your prescription: but this top-proud fellow
Whom from the flow of gall I name not, but 152
From sincere motions,—by intelligence,
And proofs as clear as founts in July, when
We see each grain of gravel,—I do know
To be corrupt and treasonous.
  Nor.   Say not 'treasonous.' 156
  Buck. To the king I'll say 't; and make my vouch as strong
As shore of rock. Attend. This holy fox,

---

138 Ipswich; *cf. n.*
153 motions: *motives*
151 top-proud: *supremely insolent*
157 vouch: *proof*

King Henry the Eighth, I. i.

Or wolf, or both,—for he is equal ravenous
As he is subtle, and as prone to mischief   160
As able to perform 't, his mind and place
Infecting one another, yea, reciprocally,
Only to show his pomp as well in France
As here at home, suggests the king our master   164
To this last costly treaty: th' interview,
That swallow'd so much treasure, and like a glass
Did break i' the rinsing.
   Nor.   Faith, and so it did.
   Buck. Pray give me favour, sir. This cunning cardinal   168
The articles o' the combination drew
As himself pleas'd; and they were ratified
As he cried, 'Thus let be,' to as much end
As give a crutch to the dead. But our count-cardinal   172
Has done this, and 'tis well; for worthy Wolsey,
Who cannot err, he did it. Now this follows,—
Which, as I take it, is a kind of puppy
To the old dam, treason,—Charles the emperor,   176
Under pretence to see the queen his aunt,
For 'twas indeed his colour, but he came
To whisper Wolsey,—here makes visitation:
His fears were that the interview betwixt   180
England and France might, through their amity,
Breed him some prejudice; for from this league
Peep'd harms that menac'd him. He privily
Deals with our cardinal, and, as I trow,—   184
Which I do well; for I am sure the emperor
Paid ere he promis'd, whereby his suit was granted
Ere it was ask'd;—but when the way was made,

---

164 suggests: *tempts*   169 combination: *agreement*
172 count-cardinal; *cf. n.*   176 Charles the emperor; *cf. n.*
178 colour: *excuse*   183 He privily; *cf. n.*

And pav'd with gold, the emperor thus desir'd: 188
That he would please to alter the king's course,
And break the foresaid peace. Let the king know—
As soon he shall by me—that thus the cardinal
Does buy and sell his honour as he pleases, 192
And for his own advantage.

  Nor.   I am sorry
To hear this of him; and could wish he were
Something mistaken in 't.

  Buck.   No, not a syllable:
I do pronounce him in that very shape 196
He shall appear in proof.

*Enter Brandon; a Sergeant-at-Arms before him, and
two or three of the Guard.*

  Bran. Your office, sergeant; execute it.
  Serg.   Sir,
My Lord the Duke of Buckingham, and Earl
Of Hereford, Stafford, and Northampton, I 200
Arrest thee of high treason, in the name
Of our most sovereign king.

  Buck.   Lo you, my lord,
The net has fall'n upon me! I shall perish
Under device and practice.

  Bran.   I am sorry 204
To see you ta'en from liberty, to look on
The business present. 'Tis his highness' pleasure
You shall to the Tower.

  Buck.   It will help me nothing
To plead mine innocence, for that dye is on me 208

---

195 mistaken: *misjudged*   197 S. d. Enter Brandon; *cf. n.*
200 Hereford; *cf. n.*   202 Lo you: *behold!*
204 device and practice: *plot and trick*
204-206 I am sorry, etc.; *cf. n.*

King Henry the Eighth, I. i.

Which makes my whit'st part black. The will of heaven
Be done in this and all things! I obey.
O, my Lord Abergavenny, fare you well!

   Bran. Nay, he must bear you company. [*To Abergavenny.*] The King
Is pleas'd you shall to the Tower, till you know
How he determines further.

   Aber.   As the duke said,
The will of heaven be done, and the king's pleasure
By me obey'd!

   Bran.   Here is a warrant from
The king t' attach Lord Montacute; and the bodies
Of the duke's confessor, John de la Car,
One Gilbert Peck, his chancellor,—

   Buck.   So, so;
These are the limbs o' the plot: no more, I hope.

   Bran. A monk o' the Chartreux.

   Buck.   O! Nicholas Hopkins?

   Bran.   He.

   Buck. My surveyor is false; the o'er-great cardinal
Hath show'd him gold. My life is spann'd already:
I am the shadow of poor Buckingham,
Whose figure even this instant cloud puts on,
By dark'ning my clear sun. My lord, farewell.

                                              Exeunt.

---

211 Lord Abergavenny; *cf. n.*
219 Gilbert Peck, his chancellor; *cf. n.*
221 Nicholas Hopkins; *cf. n.*
226 My lord; *cf. n.*

218 John de la Car; *cf. n.*
225 instant: *moment; cf. n.*

Scene Two

[*The Council Chamber*]

Cornets. Enter King Henry, leaning on the Cardinal's shoulder, the nobles and Sir Thomas Lovell; the Cardinal places himself under the King's feet on his right side.

King. My life itself, and the best heart of it,
Thanks you for this great care: I stood i' the level
Of a full-charg'd confederacy, and give thanks
To you that chok'd it. Let be call'd before us 4
That gentleman of Buckingham's; in person
I'll hear him his confessions justify;
And point by point the treasons of his master
He shall again relate. 8

A noise within, crying, 'Room for the Queen, ushered by the Duke of Norfolk.' Enter the Queen, Norfolk and Suffolk: she kneels. King riseth from his state, takes her up, kisses, and placeth her by him.

Queen. Nay, we must longer kneel: I am a suitor.
King. Arise, and take place by us: half your suit
Never name to us; you have half our power:
The other moiety, ere you ask, is given; 12
Repeat your will, and take it.
Queen.   Thank your majesty.
That you would love yourself, and in that love
Not unconsider'd leave your honour nor
The dignity of your office, is the point 16
Of my petition.

Scene Two S. d. *Cf. n.*   2 level: *range, aim*
3 confederacy: *conspiracy*
5 That . . . Buckingham's: *the surveyor*
8 S. d. Suffolk; *cf. n.*   state; *cf. n.*   12 moiety: *half*
13 Repeat your will: *say what you desire*

King Henry the Eighth, I. ii

King.   Lady mine, proceed.
Queen. I am solicited, not by a few,
And those of true condition, that your subjects
Are in great grievance: there have been commissions 20
Sent down among 'em, which hath flaw'd the heart
Of all their loyalties: wherein, although,
My good Lord Cardinal, they vent reproaches
Most bitterly on you, as putter-on   24
Of these exactions, yet the king our master,—
Whose honour heaven shield from soil!—even he
    escapes not
Language unmannerly; yea, such which breaks
The sides of loyalty, and almost appears   28
In loud rebellion.
    Nor.   Not almost appears,
It doth appear; for, upon these taxations,
The clothiers all, not able to maintain
The many to them longing, have put off   32
The spinsters, carders, fullers, weavers, who,
Unfit for other life, compell'd by hunger
And lack of other means, in desperate manner
Daring th' event to the teeth, are all in uproar,   36
And danger serves among them.
    King.   Taxation?
Wherein? and what taxation? My Lord Cardinal,
You that are blam'd for it alike with us,
Know you of this taxation?
    Car.   Please you, sir,   40
I know but of a single part in aught
Pertains to the state; and front but in that file
Where others tell steps with me.
    Queen.   No, my lord?

---

20 commissions; *cf. n.*   32 longing: *belonging*
42 front but in that file: *only march in the front rank*

You know no more than others; but you frame 44
Things that are known alike; which are not wholesome
To those which would not know them, and yet must
Perforce be their acquaintance. These exactions,
Whereof my sovereign would have note, they are 48
Most pestilent to the hearing; and to bear 'em,
The back is sacrifice to the load. They say
They are devis'd by you, or else you suffer
Too hard an exclamation.
    King.   Still exaction! 52
The nature of it? In what kind, let's know,
Is this exaction?
    Queen.   I am much too venturous
In tempting of your patience; but am bolden'd
Under your promis'd pardon. The subjects' grief 56
Comes through commissions, which compels from each
The sixth part of his substance, to be levied
Without delay; and the pretence for this
Is nam'd, your wars in France. This makes bold mouths: 60
Tongues spit their duties out, and cold hearts freeze
Allegiance in them; their curses now
Live where their prayers did; and it's come to pass,
This tractable obedience is a slave 64
To each incensed will. I would your highness
Would give it quick consideration, for
There is no primer business.
    King.   By my life,
This is against our pleasure.
    Car.   And for me, 68
I have no further gone in this than by
A single voice, and that not pass'd me but

52 exclamation: *reproach*

King Henry the Eighth, I. ii

By learned approbation of the judges. If I am
Traduc'd by ignorant tongues, which neither know 72
My faculties nor person, yet will be
The chronicles of my doing, let me say
'Tis but the fate of place, and the rough brake
That virtue must go through. We must not stint 76
Our necessary actions, in the fear
To cope malicious censurers; which ever,
As ravenous fishes, do a vessel follow
That is new-trimm'd, but benefit no further 80
Than vainly longing. What we oft do best,
By sick interpreters, once weak ones, is
Not ours, or not allow'd; what worst, as oft,
Hitting a grosser quality, is cried up 84
For our best act. If we shall stand still,
In fear our motion will be mock'd or carp'd at,
We should take root here where we sit, or sit
State-statues only.

King.   Things done well, 88
And with a care, exempt themselves from fear;
Things done without example in their issue
Are to be fear'd. Have you a precedent
Of this commission? I believe, not any. 92
We must not rend our subjects from our laws,
And stick them in our will. Sixth part of each?
A trembling contribution! Why, we take
From every tree, lop, bark, and part o' the timber; 96
And though we leave it with a root, thus hack'd,
The air will drink the sap. To every county
Where this is question'd, send our letters, with

73, 74 yet . . . doing: *yet presume to know all that I do*
78 cope: *encounter*   82 sick: *envious of us*
83 allow'd: *approved*
90 example: *precedent*   issue: *consequences*
94 stick . . . in: *make dependent upon*   will: *arbitrary caprice*
95 trembling: *tremendous, fearful*   96 lop: *branches*

Free pardon to each man that has denied 100
The force of this commission. Pray, look to 't;
I put it to your care.
   Car. [*To the Secretary.*] A word with you.
Let there be letters writ to every shire,
Of the king's grace and pardon. The griev'd commons 104
Hardly conceive of me; let it be nois'd
That through our intercession this revokement
And pardon comes: I shall anon advise you
Further in the proceeding. 108
                      Exit Secretary.
      Enter Surveyor.

   Queen. I am sorry that the Duke of Buckingham
Is run in your displeasure.
   King.   It grieves many:
The gentleman is learn'd, and a most rare speaker,
To nature none more bound; his training such 112
That he may furnish and instruct great teachers,
And never seek for aid out of himself. Yet see,
When these so noble benefits shall prove
Not well dispos'd, the mind growing once corrupt, 116
They turn to vicious forms, ten times more ugly
Than ever they were fair. This man so complete,
Who was enroll'd 'mongst wonders, and when we,
Almost with ravish'd listening, could not find 120
His hour of speech a minute; he, my lady,
Hath into monstrous habits put the graces
That once were his, and is become as black
As if besmear'd in hell. Sit by us; you shall hear—
This was his gentleman in trust—of him

105 Hardly conceive: *think hardly*
112 To . . . bound: *no one more gifted by nature*
116 dispos'd: *directed*

King Henry the Eighth, I. ii

Things to strike honour sad. Bid him recount
The fore-recited practices, whereof
We cannot feel too little, hear too much. 128

Car. Stand forth; and with bold spirit relate what you,
Most like a careful subject, have collected
Out of the Duke of Buckingham.

King.   Speak freely.

Surv. First, it was usual with him,—every day 132
It would infect his speech,—that if the king
Should without issue die, he'd carry it so
To make the sceptre his. These very words
I've heard him utter to his son-in-law, 136
Lord Abergavenny, to whom by oath he menac'd
Revenge upon the cardinal.

Car.   Please your highness, note
This dangerous conception in this point.
Not friended by his wish, to your high person 140
His will is most malignant; and it stretches
Beyond you, to your friends.

Queen.   My learn'd Lord Cardinal,
Deliver all with charity.

King.   Speak on:
How grounded he his title to the crown 144
Upon our fail? to this point hast thou heard him
At any time speak aught?

Surv.   He was brought to this
By a vain prophecy of Nicholas Henton.

King. What was that Henton?

Surv.   Sir, a Chartreux friar, 148
His confessor, who fed him every minute
With words of sovereignty.

---

127 practices: *plots*   129 Stand forth; *cf. n.*
134 carry it so: *so arrange matters as*
145 Upon our fail: *if we should die*   147 Henton; *cf. n.*

King. How know'st thou this?

Surv. Not long before your highness sped to France,
The duke being at the Rose, within the parish   152
Saint Lawrence Poultney, did of me demand
What was the speech among the Londoners
Concerning the French journey: I replied,
Men fear'd the French would prove perfidious,   156
To the king's danger.   Presently the duke
Said, 'twas the fear, indeed; and that he doubted
'Twould prove the verity of certain words
Spoke by a holy monk; 'that oft,' says he,   160
'Hath sent to me, wishing me to permit
John de la Car, my chaplain, a choice hour
To hear from him a matter of some moment:
Whom after under the confession's seal   164
He solemnly had sworn, that what he spoke,
My chaplain to no creature living but
To me should utter, with demure confidence
This pausingly ensu'd: neither the king nor 's heirs—
Tell you the duke—shall prosper: bid him strive
To [gain] the love o' the commonalty: the duke
Shall govern England.'

Queen. If I know you well,
You were the duke's surveyor, and lost your office 172
On the complaint o' the tenants: take good heed
You charge not in your spleen a noble person,
And spoil your nobler soul.   I say, take heed;
Yes, heartily beseech you.

King. Let him on.   176
Go forward.

151-171 *Cf. n.*
164 confession's seal; *cf. n.*
172 You were the duke's surveyor; *cf. n.*

157 Presently: *at once*
170 To gain; *cf. n.*
174 spleen: *malice*

King Henry the Eighth, I. ii

Surv.   On my soul, I'll speak but truth.
I told my lord the duke, by the devil's illusions
The monk might be deceiv'd; and that 'twas dangerous for him
To ruminate on this so far, until   180
It forg'd him some design, which, being believ'd,
It was much like to do. He answer'd, 'Tush!
It can do me no damage'; adding further,
That had the king in his last sickness fail'd,   184
The cardinal's and Sir Thomas Lovell's heads
Should have gone off.
    King.   Ha! what, so rank? Ah, ha!
There's mischief in this man. Canst thou say further?
    Surv. I can, my liege.
    King.   Proceed.
    Surv.   Being at Greenwich,   188
After your highness had reprov'd the duke
About Sir William Bulmer,—
    King.   I remember
Of such a time: being my sworn servant,
The duke retain'd him his. But on; what hence?   192
    Surv. 'If,' quoth he, 'I for this had been committed,
As, to the Tower, I thought, I would have play'd
The part my father meant to act upon
Th' usurper Richard; who, being at Salisbury,   196
Made suit to come in's presence; which if granted,
As he made semblance of his duty, would
Have put his knife into him.'
    King.   A giant traitor!
    Car. Now, madam, may his highness live in freedom,   200
And this man out of prison?

177-186 *Cf. n.*   179 for him; *cf. n.*   190 Bulmer; *cf. n.*
194 As . . . thought: *to the Tower, as I thought I should be*
198 would: *i.e. my father would*

Queen. God mend all!

King. There's something more would out of thee?
what sayst?

Surv. After 'the duke his father,' with 'the knife,'
He stretch'd him, and, with one hand on his
dagger, 204
Another spread on's breast, mounting his eyes,
He did discharge a horrible oath; whose tenour
Was, were he evil us'd, he would outgo
His father by as much as a performance 208
Does an irresolute purpose.

King. There's his period:
To sheathe his knife in us. He is attach'd;
Call him to present trial: if he may
Find mercy in the law, 'tis his; if none, 212
Let him not seek 't of us: by day and night!
He's traitor to the height. *Exeunt.*

Scene Three

[*A Room in the Palace*]

Enter Lord Chamberlain and Lord Sandys.

L. Ch. Is 't possible the spells of France should
juggle
Men into such strange mysteries?

L. San. New customs,
Though they be never so ridiculous,
Nay, let 'em be unmanly, yet are follow'd. 4

L. Ch. As far as I see, all the good our English
Have got by the late voyage is but merely
A fit or two o' the face; but they are shrewd ones;

---

209 period: *ultimate purpose*   213 by day and night; *cf. n.*
Scene Three; *cf.*   7 A fit . . . face: *a grimace or two*

For when they hold 'em, you would swear directly 8
Their very noses had been counsellors
To Pepin or Clotharius, they keep state so.
  L. San. They have all new legs, and lame ones: one
    would take it,
That never saw 'em pace before, the spavin 12
Or springhalt reign'd among 'em.
  L. Ch.   Death! my lord
Their clothes are after such a pagan cut too,
That, sure, they've worn out Christendom.

Enter Sir Thomas Lovell.

                                            How now!
What news, Sir Thomas Lovell?
  Lov.   Faith, my lord, 16
I hear of none but the new proclamation
That's clapp'd upon the court-gate.
  L. Ch.   What is 't for?
  Lov. The reformation of our travell'd gallants,
That fill the court with quarrels, talk, and tailors. 20
  L. Ch. I'm glad 'tis there: now I would pray our
    monsieurs
To think an English courtier may be wise,
And never see the Louvre.
  Lov.   They must either—
For so run the conditions—leave those remnants 24
Of fool and feather that they got in France,
With all their honourable points of ignorance
Pertaining thereunto,—as fights and fireworks;
Abusing better men than they can be, 28
Out of a foreign wisdom;—renouncing clean
The faith they have in tennis and tall stockings,

---

10 Pepin or Clotharius: *early French kings*
12, 13 spavin . . . springhalt; *cf. n.*
25 fool and feather: *light-brained folly; cf. n.*
27 fireworks; *cf. n.*   30 tall stockings; *cf. n.*

Short blister'd breeches, and those types of travel,
And understand again like honest men; 32
Or pack to their old playfellows: there, I take it,
They may, *cum privilegio,* wear away
The lag end of their lewdness, and be laugh'd at.

  L. San. 'Tis time to give 'em physic, their diseases 36
Are grown so catching.

  L. Ch.   What a loss our ladies
Will have of these trim vanities!

  Lov.   Ay, marry,
There will be woe indeed, lords: the sly whoresons
Have got a speeding trick to lay down ladies; 40
A French song and a fiddle has no fellow.

  L. San. The devil fiddle 'em! I am glad they're going:
For, sure, there's no converting of 'em: now
An honest country lord, as I am, beaten 44
A long time out of play, may bring his plainsong
And have an hour of hearing; and, by 'r lady,
Held current music too.

  L. Ch.   Well said, Lord Sandys;
Your colt's tooth is not cast yet.

  L. San.   No, my lord; 48
Nor shall not, while I have a stump.

  L. Ch.   Sir Thomas,
Whither were you a-going?

  Lov.   To the cardinal's:
Your lordship is a guest too.

  L. Ch.   O! 'tis true:
This night he makes a supper, and a great one, 52
To many lords and ladies; there will be

---

31 blister'd: *swollen, puffy*   32 understand: *an obvious pun*
34 cum privilegio: *by special privilege*
44, 45 beaten . . . play: *long ignored*   45 plainsong: *homely ditty, simple wooing*   47 Held current music: *be held fashionable*
48 colt's tooth: *youthful wildness*   52 makes: *gives*

King Henry the Eighth, I. iv

The beauty of this kingdom, I'll assure you.
  Lov. That churchman bears a bounteous mind indeed,
A hand as fruitful as the land that feeds us;   56
His dews fall everywhere.
  L. Ch.   No doubt he's noble;
He had a black mouth that said other of him.
  L. San. He may, my lord; h'as wherewithal: in him
Sparing would show a worse sin than ill doctrine: 60
Men of his way should be most liberal;
They are set here for examples.
  L. Ch.   True, they are so;
But few now give so great ones.   My barge stays;
Your lordship shall along.   Come, good Sir Thomas,   64
We shall be late else; which I would not be,
For I was spoke to, with Sir Henry Guilford,
This night to be comptrollers.
  L. San.   I am your lordship's.
            Exeunt.

Scene Four

[*The Presence-chamber in York-Place*]

Hautboys. A small table under a state for the Cardinal, a longer table for the guests. Then enter Anne Bullen, and divers other ladies and gentlemen, as guests, at one door; at another door enter Sir Henry Guilford.

  Guil. Ladies, a general welcome from his Grace
Salutes ye all; this night he dedicates
To fair content and you.   None here, he hopes,

---

58 had: *would have*   59 h'as: *he has*
63 My barge stays; *cf. n.*
67 comptrollers: *masters of ceremonies*   Scene Four; *cf. n.*

In all this noble bevy, has brought with her 4
One care abroad; he would have all as merry
As, first, good company, good wine, good welcome
Can make good people.

Enter Lord Chamberlain, Lord Sandys, and Lovell.

        O, my lord, y'are tardy!
The very thought of this fair company 8
Clapp'd wings to me.
 L. Ch. You are young, Sir Harry Guilford.
 L. San. Sir Thomas Lovell, had the cardinal
But half my lay-thoughts in him, some of these
Should find a running banquet ere they rested, 12
I think would better please 'em: by my life,
They are a sweet society of fair ones.
 Lov. O that your lordship were but now confessor
To one or two of these!
 L. San.   I would I were; 16
They should find easy penance.
 Lov.   Faith, how easy?
 L. San. As easy as a down-bed would afford it.
 L. Ch. Sweet ladies, will it please you sit? Sir Harry,
Place you that side, I'll take the charge of this; 20
His Grace is entering. Nay you must not freeze;
Two women plac'd together makes cold weather:
My Lord Sandys, you are one will keep 'em waking;
Pray, sit between these ladies.
 L. San.   By my faith, 24
And thank your lordship. By your leave, sweet ladies.
If I chance to talk a little wild, forgive me;
I had it from my father.
 Anne.   Was he mad, sir?

---

12 running banquet: *slight repast, but with a pun*

King Henry the Eighth, I. iv

 L. San. O very mad, exceeding mad; in love too: 28
But he would bite none; just as I do now,
He would kiss you twenty with a breath.

            [Kisses her.]
 L. Ch.   Well said, my lord.
So, now y' are fairly seated. Gentlemen,
The penance lies on you, if these fair ladies   32
Pass away frowning.
 L. San.   For my little cure,
Let me alone.

  Hautboys. Enter Cardinal Wolsey and takes
      his state.

 Car. Y' are welcome, my fair guests: that noble lady,
Or gentleman, that is not freely merry,   36
Is not my friend. This, to confirm my welcome;
And to you all, good health.   *[Drinks.]*
 L. San.   Your Grace is noble:
Let me have such a bowl may hold my thanks,
And save me so much talking.
 Car.   My lord Sandys, 40
I am beholding to you: cheer your neighbours.
Ladies, you are not merry: gentlemen,
Whose fault is this?
 L. San.   The red wine first must rise
In their fair cheeks, my lord; then we shall have 'em   44
Talk us to silence.
 Anne.   You are a merry gamester,
My Lord Sandys.
 L. San.   Yes, if I make my play.

---

30 Well said: *that's right*   33 cure: *remedy (?); charge (?)*
39 may: *as may be large enough to*
41 beholding: *indebted*   46 make my play: *win*

Here's to your ladyship; and pledge it, madam,
For 'tis to such a thing,—
    Anne.   You cannot show me.   48
    L. San. I told your Grace they would talk anon.
             Drum and trumpet; chambers discharged.
    Car.   What's that?
    L. Ch. Look out there, some of ye.
    Car.   What warlike voice,
And to what end, is this? Nay, ladies, fear not;
By all the laws of war y' are privileg'd.   52

                Enter a servant.

    L. Ch. How now, what is 't?
    Serv.   A noble troop of strangers;
For so they seem: they've left their barge and landed;
And hither make, as great ambassadors
From foreign princes.
    Car.   Good Lord Chamberlain,   56
Go, give 'em welcome; you can speak the French tongue;
And, pray, receive 'em nobly, and conduct 'em
Into our presence, where this heaven of beauty
Shall shine at full upon them. Some attend him.   60
                All rise, and tables removed.
You have now a broken banquet; but we'll mend it.
A good digestion to you all; and once more
I shower a welcome on ye; welcome all.

Hautboys. Enter King, and Others, as masquers, habited like shepherds, ushered by the Lord Chamberlain. They pass directly before the Cardinal, and gracefully salute him.

A noble company! what are their pleasures?   64

49 S. d. chambers discharged: *small cannon fired; cf. n.*

King Henry the Eighth, I. iv

L. Ch. Because they speak no English, thus they
   pray'd
To tell your Grace: that, having heard by fame
Of this so noble and so fair assembly
This night to meet here, they could do no less, 68
Out of the great respect they bear to beauty,
But leave their flocks; and, under your fair conduct,
Crave leave to view these ladies, and entreat
An hour of revels with 'em.
   Car.   Say, Lord Chamberlain, 72
They have done my poor house grace; for which I
   pay 'em
A thousand thanks, and pray 'em take their pleasures.
      Choose ladies. The King and Anne Bullen.
   King. The fairest hand I ever touch'd! O beauty,
Till now I never knew thee!   *Music. Dance.* 76
   Car. My lord.
   L. Ch.   Your Grace?
   Car.   Pray tell 'em thus much from me:
There should be one amongst 'em, by his person,
More worthy this place than myself; to whom,
If I but knew him, with my love and duty   80
I would surrender it.
   L. Ch.   I will, my lord.   *Whisper.*
   Car. What say they?
   L. Ch.   Such a one, they all confess,
There is indeed; which they would have your Grace
Find out, and he will take it.
   Car.   Let me see then.   84
By all your good leaves, gentlemen, here I'll make
My royal choice.
   King.   Ye have found him, cardinal.
You hold a fair assembly; you do well, lord:

---

75 The fairest hand; *cf.* к.

You are a churchman, or, I'll tell you, cardinal, 88
I should judge now unhappily.
 Car.   I am glad
Your Grace is grown so pleasant.
 King.   My Lord Chamberlain,
Prithee, come hither. What fair lady's that?
 L. Ch. An't please your Grace, Sir Thomas Bullen's daughter, 92
The Viscount Rochford, one of her highness' women.
 King. By heaven, she is a dainty one. Sweetheart,
I were unmannerly to take you out,
And not to kiss you. A health, gentlemen! 96
Let it go round.
 Car. Sir Thomas Lovell, is the banquet ready
I' the privy chamber?
 Lov.   Yes, my lord.
 Car.   Your Grace,
I fear, with dancing is a little heated. 100
 King. I fear, too much.
 Car.   There's fresher air, my lord,
In the next chamber.
 King. Lead in your ladies, every one. Sweet partner,
I must not yet forsake you. Let's be merry: 104
Good my Lord Cardinal, I have half a dozen healths
To drink to these fair ladies, and a measure
To lead 'em once again; and then let's dream
Who's best in favour. Let the music knock it. 108
         Exeunt with trumpets.

---

89 unhappily: *censoriously; i.e. I should think you flirtatious*
90 pleasant: *light-hearted, humorous*
92, 93 Sir Thomas . . . Rochford: *daughter of Sir Thomas Bullen, Viscount Rochford*
95 take you out: *choose you as dancing partner*
96 And . . . kiss you; *cf. n.*   106 measure: *stately dance*
108 knock it: *strike up*

King Henry the Eighth, II. i

ACT SECOND

Scene One

[*Westminster. A Street*]

Enter two Gentlemen at several doors.

1. Gent. Whither away so fast?
2. Gent. O! God save ye.
E'en to the hall, to hear what shall become
Of the great Duke of Buckingham.
1. Gent. I'll save you
That labour, sir. All's now done but the ceremony 4
Of bringing back the prisoner.
2. Gent. Were you there?
1. Gent. Yes, indeed, was I.
2. Gent. Pray speak what has happen'd.
1. Gent. You may guess quickly what.
2. Gent. Is he found guilty?
1. Gent. Yes, truly is he, and condemn'd upon 't. 8
2. Gent. I am sorry for 't.
1. Gent. So are a number more.
2. Gent. But, pray, how pass'd it?
1. Gent. I'll tell you in a little. The great duke
Came to the bar; where to his accusations 12
He pleaded still not guilty, and alleg'd
Many sharp reasons to defeat the law.
The king's attorney on the contrary
Urg'd on the examinations, proofs, confessions 16
Of divers witnesses, which the duke desir'd
To have brought, *vivâ voce,* to his face:
At which appear'd against him his surveyor;

Scene One; *cf. n.*   S. d. several: *different*
8 upon 't: *upon the verdict*
15 on the contrary: *on the opposite side*   18 To have brought; *cf. n.*

Sir Gilbert Peck, his chancellor; and John Car, 20
Confessor to him; with that devil-monk,
Hopkins, that made this mischief.
   2. Gent.   That was he
That fed him with his prophecies?
   1. Gent.   The same.
All these accus'd him strongly; which he fain 24
Would have flung from him, but, indeed, he could not:
And so his peers, upon this evidence,
Have found him guilty of high treason. Much
He spoke, and learnedly, for life; but all 28
Was either pitied in him or forgotten.
   2. Gent. After all this how did he bear himself?
   1. Gent. When he was brought again to the bar, to hear
His knell rung out, his judgment, he was stirr'd 32
With such an agony, he sweat extremely,
And something spoke in choler, ill and hasty:
But he fell to himself again, and sweetly
In all the rest show'd a most noble patience. 36
   2. Gent. I do not think he fears death.
   1. Gent.   Sure, he does not;
He never was so womanish; the cause
He may a little grieve at.
   2. Gent.   Certainly
The cardinal is the end of this.
   1. Gent.   'Tis likely 40
By all conjectures: first, Kildare's attainder,
Then deputy of Ireland; who remov'd,
Earl Surrey was sent thither, and in haste too,
Lest he should help his father.
   2. Gent.   That trick of state 44
Was a deep envious one.

43, 44 Earl Surrey . . . his father; *cf. n.*   45 envious: *malicious*

King Henry the Eighth, II. i

1. Gent.   At his return,
No doubt he will requite it. This is noted,
And generally, whoever the king favours,
The cardinal instantly will find employment,   48
And far enough from court too.
  2. Gent.   All the commons
Hate him perniciously, and o' my conscience,
Wish him ten fathom deep: this duke as much
They love and dote on; call him bounteous Bucking-
    ham,   52
The mirror of all courtesy—

Enter Buckingham from his arraignment—Tipstaves before him; the axe with the edge towards him; halberds on each side—accompanied with Sir Thomas Lovell, Sir Nicholas Vaux, Sir William Sandys, and common people, etc.

  1. Gent.   Stay there, sir,
And see the noble ruin'd man you speak of.
  2. Gent. Let's stand close, and behold him.
  Buck.   All good people,
You that thus far have come to pity me,   56
Hear what I say, and then go home and lose me.
I have this day receiv'd a traitor's judgment,
And by that name must die: yet heaven bear witness,
And if I have a conscience, let it sink me,   60
Even as the axe falls, if I be not faithful!
The law I bear no malice for my death,
'T has done upon the premises but justice;
But those that sought it I could wish more Chris-
    tians: 64

---

50 perniciously: *with a deadly hatred*
53 mirror of all courtesy; *cf. n.*
53 S. d. with the edge towards him; *cf. n.*   Sir William Sandys;
   cf. n.   57 lose: *forget*
62 bear no malice: *do not blame*

Be what they will, I heartily forgive 'em.
Yet let 'em look they glory not in mischief,
Nor build their evils on the graves of great men;
For then my guiltless blood must cry against 'em.   68
For further life in this world I ne'er hope,
Nor will I sue, although the king have mercies
More than I dare make faults. You few that lov'd me,
And dare be bold to weep for Buckingham,   72
His noble friends and fellows, whom to leave
Is only bitter to him, only dying,
Go with me, like good angels, to my end;
And as the long divorce of steel falls on me,   76
Make of your prayers one sweet sacrifice,
And lift my soul to heaven. Lead on, o' God's name.

   Lov. I do beseech your Grace, for charity,
If ever any malice in your heart   80
Were hid against me, now to forgive me frankly.

   Buck. Sir Thomas Lovell, I as free forgive you
As I would be forgiven: I forgive all.
There cannot be those numberless offences   84
'Gainst me that I cannot take peace with: no black envy
Shall make my grave. Commend me to his Grace;
And if he speak of Buckingham, pray, tell him
You met him half in heaven. My vows and prayers 88
Yet are the king's; and, till my soul forsake,
Shall cry for blessings on him: may he live
Longer than I have time to tell his years!
Ever belov'd and loving may his rule be!   92
And when old time shall lead him to his end,
Goodness and he fill up one monument!

   Lov. To the water side I must conduct your Grace;

---

67 evils: *crimes; cf. n.*

King Henry the Eighth, II. i

Then give my charge up to Sir Nicholas Vaux, 96
Who undertakes you to your end.
Vaux.   Prepare there!
The duke is coming. See the barge be ready;
And fit it with such furniture as suits
The greatness of his person.
Buck.   Nay, Sir Nicholas, 100
Let it alone; my state now will but mock me.
When I came hither, I was Lord High Constable,
And Duke of Buckingham; now poor Edward Bohun:
Yet I am richer than my base accusers, 104
That never knew what truth meant: I now seal it;
And with that blood will make 'em one day groan for 't.
My noble father, Henry of Buckingham,
Who first rais'd head against usurping Richard, 108
Flying for succour to his servant Banister,
Being distress'd, was by that wretch betray'd,
And without trial fell: God's peace be with him!
Henry the Seventh succeeding, truly pitying 112
My father's loss, like a most royal prince,
Restor'd me to my honours, and, out of ruins,
Made my name once more noble. Now his son,
Henry the Eighth, life, honour, name, and all 116
That made me happy, at one stroke has taken
For ever from the world. I had my trial,
And must needs say, a noble one; which makes me
A little happier than my wretched father: 120
Yet thus far we are one in fortunes; both
Fell by our servants, by those men we lov'd most:
A most unnatural and faithless service!

---

103 Edward Bohun; *cf. n.*   105 seal it: *i.e. with my blood*
107 My noble father; *cf. n.*   108 head: *an armed force*

Heaven has an end in all; yet, you that hear me, 124
This from a dying man receive as certain:
Where you are liberal of your loves and counsels
Be sure you be not loose; for those you make friends
And give your hearts to, when they once perceive 128
The least rub in your fortunes, fall away
Like water from ye, never found again
But where they mean to sink ye. All good people,
Pray for me! I must now forsake ye: the last hour 132
Of my long weary life is come upon me.
Farewell:
And when you would say something that is sad,
Speak how I fell. I have done; and God forgive me! 136

Exeunt Duke and Train.

1. Gent. O this is full of pity! Sir, it calls,
I fear, too many curses on their heads
That were the authors.

2. Gent. If the duke be guiltless,
'Tis full of woe; yet I can give you inkling 140
Of an ensuing evil, if it fall,
Greater than this.

1. Gent. Good angels keep it from us!
What may it be? You do not doubt my faith, sir?

2. Gent. This secret is so weighty, 'twill require 144
A strong faith to conceal it.

1. Gent. Let me have it;
I do not talk much.

2. Gent. I am confident:
You shall, sir. Did you not of late days hear

127 loose: *careless*   129 rub: *obstacle*
147 shall: *shall hear it*

A buzzing of a separation 148
Between the king and Katharine?
  1. Gent.   Yes, but it held not;
For when the king once heard it, out of anger
He sent command to the lord mayor straight
To stop the rumour, and allay those tongues 152
That durst disperse it.
  2. Gent.   But that slander, sir,
Is found a truth now; for it grows again
Fresher than e'er it was; and held for certain
The king will venture at it. Either the cardinal, 156
Or some about him near, have, out of malice
To the good queen, possess'd him with a scruple
That will undo her. To confirm this too,
Cardinal Campeius is arriv'd, and lately; 160
As all think, for this business.
  1. Gent.   'Tis the cardinal;
And merely to revenge him on the emperor
For not bestowing on him, at his asking,
The archbishopric of Toledo, this is purpos'd. 164
  2. Gent. I think you have hit the mark: but is't not cruel
That she should feel the smart of this? The cardinal
Will have his will, and she must fall.
  1. Gent.   'Tis woeful.
We are too open here to argue this! 168
Let's think in private more.   *Exeunt.*

148-153 *Cf. n.*   152 allay: *quiet*
160 Cardinal Campeius; *cf. n.*
164 The archbishopric of Toledo; *cf. n.*

Scene Two

[*An antechamber in the Palace*]

Enter Lord Chamberlain, reading this letter.

L. Ch. 'My lord, The horses your lordship sent for, with all the care I had, I saw well chosen, ridden, and furnished. They were young and handsome, and of the best breed in the north. When they were ready to set out for London, a man of my Lord Cardinal's, by commission and main power, took 'em from me; with this reason: His master would be served before a subject, if not before the king; which stopped our mouths, sir.'
I fear he will indeed. Well, let him have them:
He will have all, I think.

Enter to the Lord Chamberlain the Dukes of Norfolk and Suffolk.

Nor. Well met, my Lord Chamberlain.
L. Ch. Good day to both your Graces.
Suf. How is the king employ'd?
L. Ch.   I left him private,
Full of sad thoughts and troubles.
Nor.   What's the cause?
L. Ch. It seems the marriage with his brother's wife
Has crept too near his conscience.
Suf.   No; his conscience
Has crept too near another lady.
Nor.   'Tis so:
This is the cardinal's doing: the king-cardinal,
That blind priest, like the eldest son of Fortune,

18, 19 No . . . lady; *cf. n.*   21 blind; *cf. n.*

Turns what he list. The king will know him one day.
  Suf. Pray God he do! he'll never know himself else.
  Nor. How holily he works in all his business,   24
And with what zeal! for, now he has crack'd the league
Between us and the emperor, the queen's great nephew,
He dives into the king's soul, and there scatters
Dangers, doubts, wringing of the conscience,   28
Fears, and despairs; and all these for his marriage:
And out of all these, to restore the king,
He counsels a divorce; a loss of her,
That like a jewel has hung twenty years   32
About his neck, yet never lost her lustre;
Of her that loves him with that excellence
That angels love good men with; even of her,
That, when the greatest stroke of fortune falls,   36
Will bless the king: and is not this course pious?
  L. Ch. Heaven keep me from such counsel! 'Tis most true
These news are everywhere; every tongue speaks 'em,
And every true heart weeps for 't. All that dare   40
Look into these affairs see this main end,
The French king's sister. Heaven will one day open
The king's eyes, that so long have slept upon
This bold bad man.
  Suf.   And free us from his slavery.   44
  Nor. We had need pray,
And heartily, for our deliverance;
Or this imperious man will work us all
From princes into pages. All men's honours   48
Lie like one lump before him, to be fashion'd
Into what pitch he please.

50 pitch: *height* (?), *black defilement* (?)

Suf.   For me, my lords,
I love him not, nor fear him; there's my creed.
As I am made without him, so I'll stand,   52
If the king please; his curses and his blessings
Touch me alike, they're breath I not believe in.
I knew him, and I know him; so I leave him
To him that made him proud, the pope.
   Nor.   Let's in; 56
And with some other business put the king
From these sad thoughts, that work too much upon him.
My lord, you'll bear us company?
   L. Ch.   Excuse me;
The king has sent me otherwhere: besides,   60
You'll find a most unfit time to disturb him:
Health to your lordships.
   Nor.   Thanks, my good Lord Chamberlain.
     Exit Lord Chamberlain, and the King draws
          the curtain and sits reading pensively.
   Suf. How sad he looks! sure, he is much afflicted.
   King. Who's there? Ha?
   Nor.   Pray God he be not angry. 64
   King. Who's there, I say? How dare you thrust yourselves
Into my private meditations?
Who am I? Ha?
   Nor. A gracious king that pardons all offences   68
Malice ne'er meant: our breach of duty this way
Is business of estate; in which we come
To know your royal pleasure.
   King.   Ye are too bold.
Go to; I'll make ye know your times of business.   72
Is this an hour for temporal affairs? Ha?

62 S. d. *Cf. n.*   70 estate: *state*

King Henry the Eighth, II. ii

Enter Wolsey and Campeius with a commission.

Who's there? my good Lord Cardinal? O, my Wolsey,
The quiet of my wounded conscience!
Thou art a cure fit for a king. [*To Campeius.*] You're welcome, 76
Most learned reverend sir, into our kingdom:
Use us, and it. [*To Wolsey.*] My good lord, have great care
I be not found a talker.

Wol.   Sir, you cannot.
I would your Grace would give us but an hour 80
Of private conference.

King. [*To Norfolk and Suffolk.*] We are busy: go.

Nor. [*Aside to Suffolk.*] This priest has no pride in him!

Suf. [*Aside to Norfolk.*]   Not to speak of;
I would not be so sick though for his place:
But this cannot continue.

Nor. [*Aside to Suffolk.*] If it do, 84
I'll venture one have-at-him.

Suf. [*Aside to Norfolk.*] I another.

Exeunt Norfolk and Suffolk.

Wol. Your Grace has given a precedent of wisdom
Above all princes, in committing freely
Your scruple to the voice of Christendom. 88
Who can be angry now? what envy reach you?
The Spaniard, tied by blood and favour to her,
Must now confess, if they have any goodness,
The trial just and noble. All the clerks, 92
I mean the learned ones, in Christian kingdoms
Have their free voices. Rome, the nurse of judgment,
Invited by your noble self, hath sent

---

79 talker: *boaster, i.e. he means what he says*
83 sick: *sick with pride*   85 have-at-him; *cf. n.*

One general tongue unto us, this good man, 96
This just and learned priest, Cardinal Campeius;
Whom once more I present unto your highness.

King. And once more in mine arms I bid him welcome,
And thank the holy conclave for their loves: 100
They have sent me such a man I would have wish'd for.

Cam. Your Grace must needs deserve all strangers' loves,
You are so noble. To your highness' hand
I tender my commission, by whose virtue,— 104
The court of Rome commanding,—you, my Lord
Cardinal of York, are join'd with me, their servant,
In the unpartial judging of this business.

King. Two equal men. The queen shall be acquainted 108
Forthwith for what you come. Where's Gardiner?

Wol. I know your majesty has always lov'd her
So dear in heart, not to deny her that
A woman of less place might ask by law: 112
Scholars, allow'd freely to argue for her.

King. Ay, and the best she shall have; and my favour
To him that does best: God forbid else. Cardinal,
Prithee, call Gardiner to me, my new secretary: 116
I find him a fit fellow.

Enter Gardiner.

Wol. [*Aside to Gardiner.*] Give me your hand; much joy and favour to you;
You are the king's now.

---

100 holy conclave: *the college of Cardinals*
107 unpartial: *impartial*
109 Gardiner; *cf. n.*

108 equal: *just*
112 *Cf. n.*

King Henry the Eighth, II. ii

Gard. [*Aside to Wolsey.*] But to be commanded
For ever by your Grace, whose hand has rais'd me. 120
King. Come hither, Gardiner.

      Walks and whispers [*with Gardiner*].

Cam. My Lord of York, was not one Doctor Pace
In this man's place before him?
Wol.   Yes, he was.
Cam. Was he not held a learned man?
Wol.   Yes, surely. 124
Cam. Believe me, there's an ill opinion spread then
Even of yourself, Lord Cardinal.
Wol.   How? of me?
Cam. They will not stick to say, you envied him,
And fearing he would rise, he was so virtuous, 128
Kept him a foreign man still, which so griev'd him
That he ran mad and died.
Wol.   Heaven's peace be with him!
That's Christian care enough: for living murmurers
There's places of rebuke. He was a fool, 132
For he would needs be virtuous. That good fellow,
If I command him, follows my appointment:
I will have none so near else. Learn this, brother,
We live not to be grip'd by meaner persons. 136
King. Deliver this with modesty to the queen.

          Exit Gardiner.

The most convenient place that I can think of
For such receipt of learning is Blackfriars;
There ye shall meet about this weighty business. 140
My Wolsey, see it furnished. O my lord!
Would it not grieve an able man to leave

---

122 Doctor Pace; *cf. n.*
131 Christian care: *to wish him peace is all a Christian need do*
135 none . . . else: *no others so near the king*
139 Blackfriars; *cf. n.*

42   *The Life of*

So sweet a bedfellow? But, conscience, conscience!
O 'tis a tender place, and I must leave her.   144
                                           Exeunt.

Scene Three

[An Antechamber in the Queen's Apartments]

Enter Anne Bullen and an Old Lady.

Anne. Not for that neither: here's the pang that
    pinches:
His highness having liv'd so long with her, and she
So good a lady that no tongue could ever
Pronounce dishonour of her—by my life,   4
She never knew harm-doing—O! now, after
So many courses of the sun enthroned,
Still growing in a majesty and pomp, the which
To leave a thousand-fold more bitter than   8
'Tis sweet at first t' acquire: after this process
To give her the avaunt, it is a pity
Would move a monster.
    Old La.   Hearts of most hard temper
Melt and lament for her.
    Anne.   O God's will! much better 12
She ne'er had known pomp: though 't be temporal,
Yet if that quarrel, Fortune, do divorce
It from the bearer, 'tis a sufferance panging
As soul and body's severing.
    Old La.   Alas! poor lady,   16
She's a stranger now again.
    Anne.   So much the more
Must pity drop upon her. Verily,

Scene Three; *cf. n.*   1-11 *Cf. n.*
10 the avaunt: *the order to be off*
14 quarrel: *quarreler, the abstract for the concrete*
15 sufferance: *suffering*   panging: *causing pangs*

King Henry the Eighth, II. iii

I swear, 'tis better to be lowly born,
And range with humble livers in content, 20
Than to be perk'd up in a glist'ring grief
And wear a golden sorrow.

Old La. Our content
Is our best having.

Anne. By my troth and maidenhead
I would not be a queen.

Old La. Beshrew me, I would, 24
And venture maidenhead for 't; and so would you,
For all this spice of your hypocrisy.
You, that have so fair parts of woman on you,
Have too a woman's heart; which ever yet 28
Affected eminence, wealth, sovereignty:
Which, to say sooth, are blessings, and which gifts—
Saving your mincing—the capacity
Of your soft cheveril conscience would receive, 32
If you might please to stretch it.

Anne. Nay, good troth.

Old La. Yes, troth, and troth; you would not be a queen?

Anne. No, not for all the riches under heaven.

Old La. 'Tis strange: a three-pence bow'd would hire me, 36
Old as I am, to queen it. But, I pray you,
What think you of a duchess? have you limbs
To bear that load of title?

Anne. No, in truth.

Old La. Then you are weakly made. Pluck off a little: 40
I would not be a young count in your way,

---

21 perk'd up: *trimmed out*   23 having: *possession*
32 cheveril: *kid-leather, a type of flexibility*
36 bow'd: *made crooked, worthless; cf. n.*
40 Pluck off a little: *come down to a lower rank*

For more than blushing comes to: if your back
Cannot vouchsafe this burthen, 'tis too weak
Ever to get a boy.
   Anne.   How you do talk!
I swear again, I would not be a queen
For all the world.
   Old La.   In faith, for little England
You'd venture an emballing: I myself
Would for Carnarvonshire, although there 'long'd
No more to the crown but that. Lo! who comes here?

Enter Lord Chamberlain.

   L. Ch. Good morrow, ladies. What were 't worth to know
The secret of your conference?
   Anne.   My good lord,
Not your demand; it values not your asking:
Our mistress' sorrows we were pitying.
   L. Ch. It was a gentle business, and becoming
The action of good women: there is hope
All will be well.
   Anne.   Now, I pray God, amen!
   L. Ch. You bear a gentle mind, and heavenly blessings
Follow such creatures. That you may, fair lady,
Perceive I speak sincerely, and high note's
Ta'en of your many virtues, the king's majesty
Commends his good opinion of you, and
Does purpose honour to you no less flowing
Than Marchioness of Pembroke; to which title

---

43 vouchsafe: *be willing to accept*
44 Ever to get a boy; *cf. n.*
46 little England; *cf. n.*
47 emballing; *cf. n.*
48 Carnarvonshire; *cf. n.*
52 Not your demand: *not worth your question*
61 Commends: *sends to you; cf. n.*
63 Marchioness of Pembroke; *cf. n.*

King Henry the Eighth, II. iii

A thousand pound a year, annual support, 64
Out of his grace he adds.
 Anne. I do not know
What kind of my obedience I should tender.
More than my all is nothing, nor my prayers
Are not words duly hallow'd, nor my wishes 68
More worth than empty vanities; yet prayers and wishes
Are all I can return. Beseech your lordship,
Vouchsafe to speak my thanks and my obedience,
As from a blushing handmaid, to his highness, 72
Whose health and royalty I pray for.
 L. Ch. Lady,
I shall not fail t' approve the fair conceit
The king hath of you. [*Aside.*] I have perus'd her well;
Beauty and honour in her are so mingled 76
That they have caught the king; and who knows yet
But from this lady may proceed a gem
To lighten all this isle? [*To her.*] I'll to the king,
And say I spoke with you.
 Anne. My honour'd lord. 80
  Exit Lord Chamberlain.
 Old La. Why, this it is; see, see!
I have been begging sixteen years in court,
Am yet a courtier beggarly, nor could
Come pat betwixt too early and too late 84
For any suit of pounds; and you, O fate!
A very fresh-fish here—fie, fie, upon
This compell'd fortune!—have your mouth fill'd up
Before you open it.

67, 68 nor . . . not: *the usual double negative*
70 Beseech: *I beseech*
74 conceit: *opinion*
78 a gem; *cf. n.*
85 suit of pounds: *petition for money*
86 *Cf. n.*
87 compell'd: *unsought, violent*

Anne.   This is strange to me.   88
Old La. How tastes it? is it bitter? forty pence, no.
There was a lady once,—'tis an old story,—
That would not be a queen, that would she not
For all the mud in Egypt: have you heard it?   92
    Anne. Come, you are pleasant.
    Old La.   With your theme I could
O'ermount the lark. The Marchioness of Pembroke!
A thousand pounds a year, for pure respect!
No other obligation! By my life,   96
That promises moe thousands: honour's train
Is longer than his fore-skirt. By this time
I know your back will bear a duchess. Say,
Are you not stronger than you were?
    Anne.   Good lady, 100
Make yourself mirth with your particular fancy,
And leave me out on 't. Would I had no being,
If this salute my blood a jot: it faints me,
To think what follows.   104
The queen is comfortless, and we forgetful
In our long absence. Pray, do not deliver
What here you've heard to her.
    Old La.   What do you think me?
                                                 Exeunt.

---

89 forty pence: *a customary amount for a wager*
92 mud in Egypt; *cf. n.*   97 moe: *other, more*
98 fore-skirt: *front of gown*
103 salute: *affect*   it faints me: *I am depressed*

King Henry the Eighth, II. iv

Scene Four

[A Hall in Blackfriars]

Trumpets, sennet, and cornets. Enter two Vergers, with short silver wands; next them, two Scribes, in the habit of doctors; after them, the Bishop of Canterbury, alone; after him, the Bishops of Lincoln, Ely, Rochester, and Saint Asaph; next them, with some small distance, follows a Gentleman bearing the purse, with the great seal, and a cardinal's hat; then two Priests, bearing each a silver cross; then a Gentleman-Usher bare-headed, accompanied with a Sergeant-at-Arms, bearing a silver mace; then two Gentlemen, bearing two great silver pillars; after them, side by side, the two Cardinals; two Noblemen with the sword and mace. The King takes place under the cloth of state; the two Cardinals sit under him as judges. The Queen takes place some distance from the King. The Bishops place themselves on each side the court, in manner of a consistory; below them, the Scribes. The Lords sit next the Bishops. The rest of the Attendants stand in convenient order about the stage.

Wol. Whilst our commission from Rome is read,
Let silence be commanded.
    King.   What's the need?
It hath already publicly been read,
And on all sides th' authority allow'd;   4
You may then spare that time.
    Wol.   Be't so. Proceed.
    Scribe. Say, Henry King of England, come into the court.

Scene Four S. d.; *cf. n.*

Crier. Henry King of England, &c.
King. Here. 8
Scribe. Say, Katharine Queen of England, come into the court.
Crier. Katharine Queen of England, &c.

The Queen makes no answer, rises out of her chair, goes about the court, comes to the King, and kneels at his feet; then speaks.

Queen. Sir, I desire you do me right and justice;
And to bestow your pity on me; for 12
I am a most poor woman, and a stranger,
Born out of your dominions; having here
No judge indifferent, nor no more assurance
Of equal friendship and proceeding. Alas, sir, 16
In what have I offended you? What cause
Hath my behaviour given to your displeasure,
That thus you should proceed to put me off
And take your good grace from me? Heaven witness, 20
I have been to you a true and humble wife,
At all times to your will conformable;
Ever in fear to kindle your dislike,
Yea, subject to your countenance, glad or sorry 24
As I saw it inclin'd. When was the hour
I ever contradicted your desire,
Or made it not mine too? Or which of your friends
Have I not strove to love, although I knew 28
He were mine enemy? What friend of mine,
That had to him deriv'd your anger, did I
Continue in my liking? nay, gave notice
He was from thence discharg'd. Sir, call to mind 32

---

7 &c.: *i.e. the Crier recites the formal summons*
11 Sir, I desire; *cf. n.*   15 indifferent: *impartial*
30 to him deriv'd: *drawn upon himself*

King Henry the Eighth, II. iv

That I have been your wife, in this obedience
Upward of twenty years, and have been blest
With many children by you. If, in the course
And process of this time, you can report,   36
And prove it too, against mine honour aught,
My bond to wedlock, or my love and duty,
Against your sacred person, in God's name
Turn me away; and let the foul'st contempt   40
Shut door upon me, and so give me up
To the sharp'st kind of justice. Please you, sir,
The king, your father, was reputed for
A prince most prudent, of an excellent   44
And unmatch'd wit and judgment. Ferdinand,
My father, King of Spain, was reckon'd one
The wisest prince that there had reign'd by many
A year before. It is not to be question'd   48
That they had gather'd a wise council to them
Of every realm, that did debate this business,
Who deem'd our marriage lawful. Wherefore I humbly
Beseech you, sir, to spare me, till I may   52
Be by my friends in Spain advis'd, whose counsel
I will implore. If not, i' the name of God,
Your pleasure be fulfill'd!
   Wol.   You have here, lady,—
And of your choice,—these reverend fathers; men   56
Of singular integrity and learning,
Yea, the elect o' the land, who are assembled
To plead your cause. It shall be therefore bootless
That longer you desire the court, as well   60
For your own quiet, as to rectify
What is unsettled in the king.

---

35 many children; *cf. n.*   47 by: *in the course of*
60 That . . . court: *i.e. that you request the court to delay its proceedings*

Camp. His Grace
Hath spoken well and justly. Therefore, madam,
It's fit this royal session do proceed, 64
And that, without delay, their arguments
Be now produc'd and heard.
   Queen. Lord Cardinal,
To you I speak.
   Wol. Your pleasure, madam?
   Queen. Sir,
I am about to weep; but, thinking that 68
We are a queen,—or long have dream'd so,—certain
The daughter of a king, my drops of tears
I'll turn to sparks of fire.
   Wol. Be patient yet.
   Queen. I will, when you are humble; nay, before, 72
Or God will punish me. I do believe,
Induc'd by potent circumstances, that
You are mine enemy; and make my challenge
You shall not be my judge; for it is you 76
Have blown this coal betwixt my lord and me,
Which God's dew quench! Therefore I say again,
I utterly abhor, yea, from my soul
Refuse you for my judge, whom, yet once more, 80
I hold my most malicious foe, and think not
At all a friend to truth.
   Wol. I do profess
You speak not like yourself; who ever yet
Have stood to charity, and display'd th' effects 84
Of disposition gentle, and of wisdom
O'ertopping woman's power. Madam, you do me wrong:

---

74 potent circumstances: *strong evidences*
75 challenge: *a law term still used in claiming an objection to a juryman*
78 God's dew: *i.e. of mercy*
79 abhor: *protest against*
84 stood to: *taken the side of*

King Henry the Eighth, II. iv

I have no spleen against you; nor injustice
For you or any: how far I have proceeded, 88
Or how far further shall, is warranted
By a commission from the consistory,
Yea, the whole consistory of Rome. You charge me
That I have blown this coal: I do deny it. 92
The king is present: if it be known to him
That I gainsay my deed, how may he wound,
And worthily, my falsehood; yea, as much
As you have done my truth. If he know 96
That I am free of your report, he knows
I am not of your wrong. Therefore in him
It lies to cure me; and the cure is to
Remove these thoughts from you: the which before 100
His highness shall speak in, I do beseech
You, gracious madam, to unthink your speaking,
And to say so no more.
   Queen.   My lord, my lord,
I am a simple woman, much too weak 104
To oppose your cunning. Y' are meek and humble-mouth'd;
You sign your place and calling, in full seeming,
With meekness and humility; but your heart
Is cramm'd with arrogancy, spleen, and pride. 108
You have, by fortune and his highness' favours,
Gone slightly o'er low steps, and now are mounted
Where powers are your retainers, and your words,
Domestics to you, serve your will as 't please 112
Yourself pronounce their office. I must tell you,
You tender more your person's honour than

---

101 in: *in reference to, upon*
102 unthink your speaking: *disabuse your mind of what you have said*   106 sign: *mark*   seeming: *feigning*
110 slightly: *easily*
111 powers: *powers incidental to your high offices*
111-113 your words . . . office; *cf. n.*
114 tender: *regard*

Your high profession spiritual; that again
I do refuse you for my judge; and here, 116
Before you all, appeal unto the pope,
To bring my whole cause 'fore his holiness,
And to be judg'd by him.

    She curtsies to the King, and offers to depart.
 Camp.   The queen is obstinate,
Stubborn to justice, apt to accuse it, and 120
Disdainful to be tried by 't: 'tis not well.
She's going away.
 King. Call her again.
 Crier. Katharine Queen of England, come into the court. 124
 Gent. Ush. Madam, you are call'd back.
 Queen. What need you note it? pray you, keep your way:
When you are call'd, return. Now, the Lord help!
They vex me past my patience. Pray you, pass on: 128
I will not tarry; no, nor ever more
Upon this business my appearance make
In any of their courts.

    Exeunt Queen, and her Attendants.
 King.   Go thy ways, Kate:
That man i' the world who shall report he has 132
A better wife, let him in nought be trusted,
For speaking false in that: thou art, alone,—
If thy rare qualities, sweet gentleness,
Thy meekness saintlike, wifelike government, 136
Obeying in commanding, and thy parts
Sovereign and pious else, could speak thee out,—
The queen of earthly queens. She's noble born;

120 apt: *readily inclined*   125 Gent. Ush.; *cf. n.*
136 government: *behavior*

King Henry the Eighth, II. iv

And, like her true nobility, she has 140
Carried herself towards me.
Wol.   Most gracious sir,
In humblest manner I require your highness,
That it shall please you to declare, in hearing
Of all these ears,—for where I am robb'd and bound
There must I be unloos'd, although not there
At once and fully satisfied,—whether ever I
Did broach this business to your highness, or
Laid any scruple in your way, which might 148
Induce you to the question on 't? or ever
Have to you, but with thanks to God for such
A royal lady, spake one the least word that might
Be to the prejudice of her present state, 152
Or touch of her good person?
King.   My Lord Cardinal,
I do excuse you; yea, upon mine honour,
I free you from 't. You are not to be taught
That you have many enemies, that know not 156
Why they are so, but, like to village curs,
Bark when their fellows do. By some of these
The queen is put in anger. Y' are excus'd:
But will you be more justified? You ever 160
Have wish'd the sleeping of this business; never
Desir'd it to be stirr'd; but oft have hinder'd, oft,
The passages made toward it. On my honour,
I speak my good Lord Cardinal to this point, 164
And thus far clear him. Now, what mov'd me to 't,
I will be bold with time and your attention:
Then mark th' inducement. Thus it came; give heed to 't:
My conscience first receiv'd a tenderness, 168

153 touch . . . person: *sullying of her good reputation*
164 speak: *bear witness in favor of*
166 *I ask time and your attention while I explain*

Scruple, and prick, on certain speeches utter'd
By the Bishop of Bayonne, then French ambassador,
Who had been hither sent on the debating
A marriage 'twixt the Duke of Orleans and 172
Our daughter Mary. I' the progress of this business,
Ere a determinate resolution, he—
I mean, the bishop—did require a respite,
Wherein he might the king his lord advertise 176
Whether our daughter were legitimate,
Respecting this our marriage with the dowager,
Sometimes our brother's wife. This respite shook
The bosom of my conscience, enter'd me, 180
Yea, with a splitting power, and made to tremble
The region of my breast; which forc'd such way,
That many-maz'd considerings did throng,
And press'd in with this caution. First, methought 184
I stood not in the smile of heaven, who had
Commanded nature, that my lady's womb,
If it conceiv'd a male child by me, should
Do no more offices of life to't than 188
The grave does to the dead; for her male issue
Or died where they were made, or shortly after
This world had air'd them. Hence I took a thought,
This was a judgment on me; that my kingdom, 192
Well worthy the best heir o' the world, should not
Be gladded in't by me. Then follows that
I weigh'd the danger which my realms stood in
By this my issue's fail; and that gave to me 196
Many a groaning throe. Thus hulling in
The wild sea of my conscience, I did steer
Toward this remedy, whereupon we are

---

170 Bishop of Bayonne; *cf. n.*   176 advertise: *inform*
179 Sometimes: *sometime, formerly*
180 bosom of my conscience; *cf. n.*   183 many-maz'd: *intricate*
197 hulling: *drifting without sail at the mercy of the waves*

King Henry the Eighth, II. iv

Now present here together; that's to say, 200
I meant to rectify my conscience, which
I then did feel full sick, and yet not well,
By all the reverend fathers of the land
And doctors learn'd. First, I began in private 204
With you, my Lord of Lincoln; you remember
How under my oppression I did reek,
When I first mov'd you.

Lin.   Very well, my liege.

King. I have spoke long: be pleas'd yourself to say 208
How far you satisfied me.

Lin.   So please your highness,
The question did at first so stagger me,
Bearing a state of mighty moment in 't,
And consequence of dread, that I committed 212
The daring'st counsel that I had to doubt,
And did entreat your highness to this course
Which you are running here.

King.   I then mov'd you,
My Lord of Canterbury, and got your leave 216
To make this present summons. Unsolicited
I left no reverend person in this court;
But by particular consent proceeded
Under your hands and seals; therefore go on, 220
For no dislike i' the world against the person
Of the good queen; but the sharp thorny points
Of my alleged reasons drives this forward.
Prove but our marriage lawful, by my life 224
And kingly dignity, we are contented
To wear our mortal state to come with her,
Katharine our queen, before the primest creature

---

211 state: *political issue*   223 drives: *drive; cf. n.*

That's paragon'd o' the world.
 Camp.   So please your highness, 228
The queen being absent, 'tis a needful fitness
That we adjourn this court till further day:
Meanwhile must be an earnest motion
Made to the queen, to call back her appeal   232
She intends unto his holiness.
 King.   [*Aside.*]   I may perceive
These cardinals trifle with me: I abhor
This dilatory sloth and tricks of Rome.
My learn'd and well-beloved servant Cranmer,   236
Prithee, return: with thy approach, I know,
My comfort comes along. Break up the court:
I say, set on.
      Exeunt, in manner as they entered.

ACT THIRD

Scene One

[*The Palace at Bridewell. A Room in the Queen's Apartment*]

Enter the Queen and her women as at work.

 Queen. Take thy lute, wench; my soul grows sad with troubles;
Sing and disperse 'em, if thou canst. Leave working.

SONG.

 'Orpheus with his lute made trees,
  And the mountain tops that freeze,   4

---

228 paragon'd: *set forth as a model*   236 Cranmer; *cf. n.*
Scene One; *cf. n.*

King Henry the Eighth, III. i

    Bow themselves, when he did sing:
    To his music plants and flowers
    Ever sprung, as sun and showers
      There had made a lasting spring.   8

    'Every thing that heard him play,
    Even the billows of the sea,
      Hung their heads, and then lay by.
    In sweet music is such art,   12
    Killing care and grief of heart
      Fall asleep or, hearing, die.'

Enter a Gentleman.

Queen. How now!
Gent. An't please your Grace, the two great cardinals   16
Wait in the presence.
Queen.   Would they speak with me?
Gent. They will'd me say so, Madam.
Queen.   Pray their Graces
To come near. [*Exit Gentleman.*] What can be their business
With me, a poor weak woman, fall'n from favour?   20
I do not like their coming, now I think on 't.
They should be good men, their affairs as righteous;
But all hoods make not monks.

Enter the two Cardinals, Wolsey and Campeius.

Wol.   Peace to your highness!
Queen. Your Graces find me here part of a housewife,   24
I would be all, against the worst may happen.
What are your pleasures with me, reverend lords?

---

7 as: *as if*   16 An't: *if it*   17 presence: *presence-chamber*
23 all . . . monks; *cf. n.*   24 part of: *in part*

Wol. May it please you, noble madam, to withdraw
Into your private chamber, we shall give you   28
The full cause of our coming.
    Queen.   Speak it here.
There's nothing I have done yet, o' my conscience,
Deserves a corner: would all other women
Could speak this with as free a soul as I do!   32
My lords, I care not—so much I am happy
Above a number—if my actions
Were tried by every tongue, every eye saw 'em,
Envy and base opinion set against 'em,   36
I know my life so even. If your business
Seek me out, and that way I am wife in,
Out with it boldly: truth loves open dealing.
    *Wol. Tanta est erga te mentis integritas, regina
        serenissima,—*   40
    Queen. O, good my lord, no Latin!
I am not such a truant since my coming
As not to know the language I have liv'd in:
A strange tongue makes my cause more strange, suspicious;   44
Pray, speak in English: here are some will thank you,
If you speak truth, for their poor mistress' sake:
Believe me, she has had much wrong. Lord Cardinal,
The willing'st sin I ever yet committed   48
May be absolv'd in English.
    Wol.   Noble lady,
I am sorry my integrity should breed,—
And service to his majesty and you,—
So deep suspicion, where all faith was meant.   52
We come not by the way of accusation,
To taint that honour every good tongue blesses,

27 May it: *if it may*
38 that way I am wife in: *i.e. how I behave as a wife*   40 *Cf. n.*

King Henry the Eighth, III. i

Nor to betray you any way to sorrow;—
You have too much, good lady: but to know 56
How you stand minded in the weighty difference
Between the king and you; and to deliver,
Like free and honest men, our just opinions
And comforts to your cause.
   Camp.   Most honour'd madam, 60
My Lord of York, out of his noble nature,
Zeal and obedience he still bore your Grace,
Forgetting, like a good man, your late censure
Both of his truth and him,—which was too far,— 64
Offers, as I do, in a sign of peace,
His service and his counsel.
   Queen.   [*Aside.*] To betray me.
My lords, I thank you both for your good wills;
Ye speak like honest men,—pray God, ye prove so!— 68
But how to make ye suddenly an answer
In such a point of weight, so near mine honour,—
More near my life, I fear,—with my weak wit,
And to such men of gravity and learning, 72
In truth I know not. I was set at work
Among my maids; full little, God knows, looking
Either for such men or such business.
For her sake that I have been,—for I feel 76
The last fit of my greatness,—good your Graces,
Let me have time and counsel for my cause:
Alas! I am a woman, friendless, hopeless.
   Wol. Madam, you wrong the king's love with these fears: 80
Your hopes and friends are infinite.
   Queen.   In England
But little for my profit. Can you think, lords,

60 your cause; *cf. n.*   73 was set: *was sitting*

That any Englishman dare give me counsel?
Or be a known friend, 'gainst his highness' pleasure,—
Though he be grown so desperate to be honest,—
And live a subject? Nay, forsooth, my friends,
They that must weigh out my afflictions,
They that my trust must grow to, live not here: 88
They are, as all my other comforts, far hence
In mine own country, lords.
   Camp.   I would your Grace
Would leave your griefs, and take my counsel.
   Queen.   How, sir?
   Camp. Put your main cause into the king's protection; 92
He's loving and most gracious: 'twill be much
Both for your honour better and your cause;
For if the trial of the law o'ertake ye,
You'll part away disgrac'd.
   Wol.   He tells you rightly. 96
   Queen. Ye tell me what ye wish for both: my ruin.
Is this your Christian counsel? out upon ye!
Heaven is above all yet; there sits a judge
That no king can corrupt.
   Camp.   Your rage mistakes us. 100
   Queen. The more shame for ye! holy men I thought ye,
Upon my soul, two reverend cardinal virtues;
But cardinal sins and hollow hearts I fear ye.
Mend 'em, for shame, my lords. Is this your comfort? 104
The cordial that ye bring a wretched lady,
A woman lost among ye, laugh'd at, scorn'd?
I will not wish ye half my miseries,

---

85 so . . . honest: *so reckless as to be honest*
87 weigh out: *outweigh* (?), *ponder* (?)

I have more charity; but say, I warn'd ye: 108
Take heed, for heaven's sake, take heed, lest at once
The burthen of my sorrows fall upon ye.

Wol. Madam, this is a mere distraction;
You turn the good we offer into envy. 112

Queen. Ye turn me into nothing: woe upon ye,
And all such false professors! Would you have me—
If you have any justice, any pity;
If ye be anything but churchmen's habits— 116
Put my sick cause into his hands that hates me?
Alas! h'as banish'd me his bed already,
His love too long ago! I am old, my lords,
And all the fellowship I hold now with him 120
Is only my obedience. What can happen
To me above this wretchedness? all your studies
Make me a curse like this.

Camp. Your fears are worse.

Queen. Have I liv'd thus long—let me speak myself, 124
Since virtue finds no friends—a wife, a true one?
A woman, I dare say without vainglory,
Never yet branded with suspicion?
Have I with all my full affections 128
Still met the king? lov'd him next heaven? obey'd him?
Been, out of fondness, superstitious to him?
Almost forgot my prayers to content him?
And am I thus rewarded? 'Tis not well, lords. 132
Bring me a constant woman to her husband,
One that ne'er dreamed a joy beyond his pleasure,
And to that woman, when she has done most,
Yet will I add an honour, a great patience. 136

---

112 envy: *malice*　　　　　　　124 speak myself; *cf. II. iv. 164*
133 a constant . . . husband: *a woman constant to her husband*

Wol. Madam, you wander from the good we aim at.
Queen. My lord, I dare not make myself so guilty,
To give up willingly that noble title
Your master wed me to: nothing but death   140
Shall e'er divorce my dignities.
    Wol.   Pray hear me.
    Queen. Would I had never trod this English earth,
Or felt the flatteries that grow upon it!   143
Ye have angels' faces, but heaven knows your hearts.
What will become of me now, wretched lady?
I am the most unhappy woman living.
[*To her women.*] Alas! poor wenches, where are now your fortunes?
Shipwrack'd upon a kingdom, where no pity,   148
No friends, no hope; no kindred weep for me;
Almost no grave allow'd me. Like the lily,
That once was mistress of the field and flourish'd,
I'll hang my head and perish.
    Wol.   If your Grace   152
Could but be brought to know our ends are honest,
You'd feel more comfort. Why should we, good lady,
Upon what cause, wrong you? alas! our places,
The way of our profession is against it: 156
We are to cure such sorrows, not to sow 'em.
For goodness' sake, consider what you do;
How you may hurt yourself, ay, utterly
Grow from the king's acquaintance, by this **carriage**.
The hearts of princes kiss obedience,
So much they love it; but to stubborn spirits
They swell, and grow as terrible as storms.
I know you have a gentle, noble temper,   164
A soul as even as a calm: pray think us

---

144 angels' faces; *cf. n.*   160 carriage: *behavior*

King Henry the Eighth, III. ii

Those we profess, peace-makers, friends, and servants.

Camp. Madam, you'll find it so. You wrong your virtues
With these weak women's fears: a noble spirit, 168
As yours was put into you, ever casts
Such doubts, as false coin, from it. The king loves you;
Beware you lose it not: for us, if you please
To trust us in your business, we are ready 172
To use our utmost studies in your service.

Queen. Do what ye will, my lords: and, pray, forgive me,
If I have us'd myself unmannerly.
You know I am a woman, lacking wit 176
To make a seemly answer to such persons.
Pray do my service to his majesty:
He has my heart yet; and shall have my prayers
While I shall have my life. Come, reverend fathers,
Bestow your counsels on me. She now begs 181
That little thought, when she set footing here,
She should have bought her dignities so dear.

Exeunt.

Scene Two

[Antechamber to the King's Apartment]

Enter the Duke of Norfolk, Duke of Suffolk, Lord Surrey, and Lord Chamberlain.

Nor. If you will now unite in your complaints,
And force them with a constancy, the cardinal
Cannot stand under them. If you omit

166 Those we profess: *what we profess to be*
Scene Two; *cf. n.*

175 us'd: *behaved*
2 force: *urge*

The offer of this time, I cannot promise 4
But that you shall sustain moe new disgraces
With these you bear already.
   Sur.   I am joyful
To meet the least occasion that may give me
Remembrance of my father-in-law, the duke, 8
To be reveng'd on him.
   Suf.   Which of the peers
Have uncontemn'd gone by him, or at least
Strangely neglected? When did he regard
The stamp of nobleness in any person, 12
Out of himself?
   L. Ch.   My lords, you speak your pleasures:
What he deserves of you and me, I know;
What we can do to him,—though now the time
Gives way to us,—I much fear. If you cannot 16
Bar his access to the king, never attempt
Anything on him, for he hath a witchcraft
Over the king in's tongue.
   Nor.   O fear him not!
His spell in that is out: the king hath found 20
Matter against him that for ever mars
The honey of his language. No, he's settled,
Not to come off, in his displeasure.
   Sur.   Sir,
I should be glad to hear such news as this 24
Once every hour.
   Nor.   Believe it, this is true.
In the divorce his contrary proceedings
Are all unfolded; wherein he appears
As I would wish mine enemy.
   Sur.   How came 28

8 my father-in-law, the duke: *i.e. the Duke of Buckingham*
13 Out of: *except*   16 Gives way to us: *favors us*
23 Not to come off; *cf. n.*   26 contrary: *inconsistent, devious*

His practices to light?
  Suf.   Most strangely.
  Sur.   O how? how?
  Suf. The cardinal's letters to the pope miscarried,
And came to th' eye o' the king; wherein was read,
How that the cardinal did entreat his holiness   32
To stay the judgment o' the divorce; for if
It did take place, 'I do,' quoth he, 'perceive
My king is tangled in affection to
A creature of the queen's, Lady Anne Bullen.'   36
  Sur. Has the king this?
  Suf.   Believe it.
  Sur.   Will this work?
  L. Ch. The king in this perceives him, how he coasts
And hedges his own way. But in this point
All his tricks founder, and he brings his physic   40
After his patient's death: the king already
Hath married the fair lady.
  Sur.   Would he had!
  Suf. May you be happy in your wish, my lord!
For I profess, you have it.
  Sur.   Now all my joy   44
Trace the conjunction!
  Suf.   My amen to 't!
  Nor.   All men's.
  Suf. There's order given for her coronation:
Marry, this is yet but young, and may be left
To some ears unrecounted. But, my lords,   48
She is a gallant creature, and complete
In mind and feature: I persuade me, from her
Will fall some blessing to this land, which shall
In it be memoriz'd.

30 *Cf. n.*   42 Would he had; *cf. n.*
45 Trace: *follow*   51 some blessing; *cf. n.*

Sur.   But will the king 52
Digest this letter of the cardinal's?
The Lord forbid!
   Nor.   Marry, amen!
   Suf.   No, no;
There be moe wasps that buzz about his nose
Will make this sting the sooner. Cardinal Campeius 56
Is stol'n away to Rome; hath ta'en no leave;
Has left the cause o' the king unhandled; and
Is posted, as the agent of our cardinal,
To second all his plot. I do assure you 60
The king cried 'Ha!' at this.
   L. Ch.   Now, God incense him,
And let him cry 'Ha!' louder.
   Nor.   But, my lord,
When returns Cranmer?
   Suf. He is return'd in his opinions, which 64
Have satisfied the king for his divorce,
Together with all famous colleges
Almost in Christendom. Shortly, I believe,
His second marriage shall be publish'd, and 68
Her coronation. Katharine no more
Shall be call'd queen, but princess dowager,
And widow to Prince Arthur.
   Nor.   This same Cranmer's
A worthy fellow, and hath ta'en much pain 72
In the king's business.
   Suf.   He has; and we shall see him
For it an archbishop.
   Nor.   So I hear.

---

53 Digest: *put up with*   56 Cardinal Campeius; *cf. n.*
64 return'd in his opinions: *i.e. having forwarded the opinions of universities he was sent to get*
69-71 Katharine . . . Arthur; *cf. n.*

King Henry the Eighth, III. ii

Suf.   'Tis so.

Enter Wolsey and Cromwell.

The cardinal!
 Nor.   Observe, observe; he's moody.
 Car. The packet, Cromwell,   76
Gave 't you the king?
 Crom. To his own hand, in's bedchamber.
 Car. Look'd he o' th' inside of the paper?
 Crom.   Presently
He did unseal them; and the first he view'd,   80
He did it with a serious mind; a heed
Was in his countenance. You he bade
Attend him here this morning.
 Car.   Is he ready
To come abroad?
 Crom.   I think, by this he is.   84
 Car. Leave me awhile.   *Exit Cromwell.*
[*Aside.*] It shall be to the Duchess of Alençon,
The French King's sister; he shall marry her.
Anne Bullen! No; I'll no Anne Bullens for him: 88
There's more in 't than fair visage. Bullen!
No, we'll no Bullens. Speedily I wish
To hear from Rome. The Marchioness of Pembroke!
 Nor. He's discontented.
 Suf.   May be he hears the king   92
Does whet his anger to him.
 Sur.   Sharp enough,
Lord, for thy justice!
 Car. The late queen's gentlewoman, a knight's daughter,
To be her mistress' mistress! the queen's queen! 96
This candle burns not clear: 'tis I must snuff it;

86 Duchess of Alencon; *cf. n.*

Then, out it goes. What though I know her virtuous
And well deserving? yet I know her for
A spleeny Lutheran; and not wholesome to   100
Our cause, that she should lie i' the bosom of
Our hard-rul'd king. Again, there is sprung up
An heretic, an arch one, Cranmer; one
Hath crawl'd into the favour of the king,   104
And is his oracle.

   Nor.   He is vex'd at something.

   Sur. I would 'twere something that would fret the string,
The master-cord on's heart!

           Enter King, reading of a schedule.

   Suf.   The king, the king!

   King. What piles of wealth hath he accumulated   108
To his own portion! and what expense by the hour
Seems to flow from him! How, i' the name of thrift,
Does he rake this together? Now, my lords,
Saw you the cardinal?

   Nor.   My lord, we have   112
Stood here observing him. Some strange commotion
Is in his brain: he bites his lip, and starts;
Stops on a sudden, looks upon the ground,
Then lays his finger on his temple; straight   116
Springs out into fast gait; then stops again,
Strikes his breast hard; and anon he casts
His eye against the moon: in most strange postures
We have seen him set himself.

   King.   It may well be,   120
There is a mutiny in's mind. This morning
Papers of state he sent me to peruse,

---

100 A spleeny Lutheran; *cf. n.*   104 Hath: *who hath*
107 S. d.; *cf. n.*

King Henry the Eighth, III. ii

As I requir'd; and wot you what I found
There, on my conscience, put unwittingly? 124
Forsooth, an inventory, thus importing:
The several parcels of his plate, his treasure,
Rich stuffs and ornaments of household, which
I find at such proud rate that it out-speaks 128
Possession of a subject.
  Nor.   It's heaven's will:
Some spirit put this paper in the packet
To bless your eye withal.
  King.   If we did think
His contemplation were above the earth, 132
And fix'd on spiritual object, he should still
Dwell in his musings: but I am afraid
His thinkings are below the moon, not worth
His serious considering.
                    King takes his seat, whispers Lovell,
                        who goes to the Cardinal.
  Car.   Heaven forgive me! 136
Ever God bless your highness!
  King.   Good my lord,
You are full of heavenly stuff, and bear the inventory
Of your best graces in your mind, the which
You were now running o'er: you have scarce time 140
To steal from spiritual leisure a brief span
To keep your earthly audit: sure, in that
I deem you an ill husband, and am glad
To have you therein my companion.
  Car.   Sir, 144
For holy offices I have a time; a time
To think upon the part of business which

128, 129 out-speaks . . . subject: *indicates more than a subject
        should possess*   131 withal: *therewith*
143 an ill husband: *a bad manager*

I bear i' the state; and nature does require
Her times of preservation, which perforce 148
I, her frail son, amongst my brethren mortal,
Must give my tendance to.
  King.   You have said well.
  Car. And ever may your highness yoke together,
As I will lend you cause, my doing well 152
With my well saying.
  King.   'Tis well said again;
And 'tis a kind of good deed to say well:
And yet words are no deeds. My father lov'd you:
He said he did, and with his deed did crown 156
His word upon you. Since I had my office,
I have kept you next my heart; have not alone
Employ'd you where high profits might come home,
But par'd my present havings, to bestow 160
My bounties upon you.
  Car.   [*Aside.*] What should this mean?
  Sur. [*Aside.*] The Lord increase this business!
  King.   Have I not made you
The prime man of the state? I pray you, tell me
If what I now pronounce you have found true; 164
And if you may confess it, say withal,
If you are bound to us or no. What say you?
  Car. My sovereign, I confess your royal graces,
Shower'd on me daily, have been more than could 168
My studied purposes requite; which went
Beyond all man's endeavours. My endeavours
Have ever come too short of my desires,
Yet fil'd with my abilities. Mine own ends 172
Have been mine so, that evermore they pointed
To the good of your most sacred person and

160 par'd . . . havings: *diminished my present possessions*
167-172 *Cf. n.*   172 fil'd: *kept pace with*
173 so: *in this sense only*

King Henry the Eighth, III. ii

The profit of the state. For your great graces
Heap'd upon me, poor undeserver, I 176
Can nothing render but allegiant thanks,
My prayers to heaven for you, my loyalty,
Which ever has and ever shall be growing,
Till death, that winter, kill it.
  King.   Fairly answer'd: 180
A loyal and obedient subject is
Therein illustrated; the honour of it
Does pay the act of it, as i' the contrary
The foulness is the punishment. I presume 184
That as my hand has open'd bounty to you,
My heart dropp'd love, my power rain'd honour, more
On you than any; so your hand and heart,
Your brain, and every function of your power, 188
Should, notwithstanding that your bond of duty,
As 'twere in love's particular, be more
To me, your friend, than any.
  Car.   I do profess,
That for your highness' good I ever labour'd 192
More than mine own; that am, have, and will be.
Though all the world should crack their duty to you,
And throw it from their soul; though perils did
Abound as thick as thought could make 'em, and 196
Appear in forms more horrid, yet my duty,
As doth a rock against the chiding flood,
Should the approach of this wild river break,
And stand unshaken yours.
  King.   'Tis nobly spoken. 200
Take notice, lords, he has a loyal breast,

---

177 allegiant: *loyal*
182, 183 the honour . . . act of it: *a loyal subject's nobility of character rewards him for his actions*
183 the contrary: *a character of the opposite nature*
189-191 Should . . . any; *cf. n.*
193 that am, have, and will be; *cf. n.*

For you have seen him open 't. Read o'er this;
                [*Giving him papers.*]
And after, this: and then to breakfast with
What appetite you have.
        *Exit King, frowning upon the Cardinal; the
           nobles throng after him, smiling and whis-
           pering.*
  Car.   What should this mean? 204
What sudden anger's this? how have I reap'd it?
He parted frowning from me, as if ruin
Leap'd from his eyes. So looks the chafed lion
Upon the daring huntsman that has gall'd him: 208
Then makes him nothing. I must read this paper;
I fear, the story of his anger. 'Tis so:
This paper has undone me! 'Tis th' account
Of all that world of wealth I have drawn together 212
For mine own ends; indeed, to gain the popedom,
And fee my friends in Rome. O negligence!
Fit for a fool to fall by: what cross devil
Made me put this main secret in the packet   216
I sent the king? Is there no way to cure this?
No new device to beat this from his brains?
I know 'twill stir him strongly; yet I know
A way, if it take right, in spite of fortune   220
Will bring me off again. What's this?—'To the Pope!'
The letter, as I live, with all the business
I writ to's holiness. Nay then, farewell!
I have touch'd the highest point of all my greatness;   224
And from that full meridian of my glory,
I haste now to my setting. I shall fall

215 cross: *perverse*   216 main: *chief*

King Henry the Eighth, III. ii

Like a bright exhalation in the evening,
And no man see me more. 228

*Enter to Wolsey the Dukes of Norfolk and Suffolk,
the Earl of Surrey, and the Lord Chamberlain.*

Nor. Hear the king's pleasure, cardinal: who commands you
To render up the great seal presently
Into our hands; and to confine yourself
To Asher-house, my Lord of Winchester's, 232
Till you hear further from his highness.
   Car.   Stay:
Where's your commission, lords? words cannot carry
Authority so weighty.
   Suf.   Who dare cross 'em,
Bearing the king's will from his mouth expressly? 236
   Car. Till I find more than will or words to do it,—
I mean your malice,—know, officious lords,
I dare and must deny it. Now I feel
Of what coarse metal ye are moulded, envy: 240
How eagerly ye follow my disgraces,
As if it fed ye! and how sleek and wanton
Ye appear in everything may bring my ruin!
Follow your envious courses, men of malice; 244
You have Christian warrant for 'em, and, no doubt,
In time will find their fit rewards. That seal
You ask with such a violence, the king—
Mine and your master—with his own hand gave me;
Bade me enjoy it with the place and honours 249
During my life; and to confirm his goodness,
Tied it by letters-patents. Now who'll take it?
   Sur. The king, that gave it.
   Car.   It must be himself then. 252

---

227 exhalation: *falling star*   232 Asher-house; *cf. n.*
240 envy: *namely, of envy*   251 letters-patents: *legal documents*

Sur. Thou art a proud traitor, priest.
Car. Proud lord, thou liest:
Within these forty hours Surrey durst better
Have burnt that tongue than said so.
Sur. Thy ambition,
Thou scarlet sin, robb'd this bewailing land 256
Of noble Buckingham, my father-in-law:
The heads of all thy brother cardinals—
With thee and all thy best parts bound together—
Weigh'd not a hair of his. Plague of your policy! 260
You sent me deputy for Ireland,
Far from his succour, from the king, from all
That might have mercy on the fault thou gav'st him;
Whilst your great goodness, out of holy pity, 264
Absolv'd him with an axe.
Car. This and all else
This talking lord can lay upon my credit,
I answer is most false. The duke by law
Found his deserts: how innocent I was 268
From any private malice in his end,
His noble jury and foul cause can witness.
If I lov'd many words, lord, I should tell you,
You have as little honesty as honour, 272
That in the way of loyalty and truth
Toward the king, my ever royal master,
Dare mate a sounder man than Surrey can be,
And all that love his follies.
Sur. By my soul, 276
Your long coat, priest, protects you; thou shouldst feel
My sword i' the life-blood of thee else. My lords,
Can ye endure to hear this arrogance?
And from this fellow? If we live thus tamely, 280
To be thus jaded by a piece of scarlet,

275 Dare mate: *I dare rival*   281 jaded: *befooled*

King Henry the Eighth, III. ii

Farewell nobility; let his Grace go forward,
And dare us with his cap like larks.
　Car.　　　　　　　　　　All goodness
Is poison to thy stomach.
　Sur.　　　　　　　Yes, that goodness　284
Of gleaning all the land's wealth into one,
Into your own hands, cardinal, by extortion:
The goodness of your intercepted packets,
You writ to the pope against the king: your goodness,　288
Since you provoke me, shall be most notorious.
My Lord of Norfolk, as you are truly noble,
As you respect the common good, the state
Of our despis'd nobility, our issues,　292
Who, if he live, will scarce be gentlemen,
Produce the grand sum of his sins, the articles
Collected from his life.　I'll startle you
Worse than the sacring bell, when the brown wench 296
Lay kissing in your arms, Lord Cardinal.
　Car. How much, methinks, I could despise this man,
But that I am bound in charity against it!
　Nor. Those articles, my lord, are in the king's hand;　300
But, thus much, they are foul ones.
　Car.　　　　　　　So much fairer
And spotless shall mine innocence arise
When the king knows my truth.
　Sur.　　　　　　　This cannot save you:
I thank my memory, I yet remember　304
Some of these articles; and out they shall.
Now, if you can blush, and cry 'guilty,' cardinal,
You'll show a little honesty.

---

283 dare: *dazzle birds with a piece of scarlet cloth, to catch them*
292 issues: *children*　　　　　　　　296 sacring bell; *cf. n.*
300 hand: *possession*

Car. Speak on, sir;
I dare your worst objections. If I blush,
It is to see a nobleman want manners.

Sur. I had rather want those than my head. Have at you!
First, that, without the king's assent or knowledge,
You wrought to be a legate, by which power
You maim'd the jurisdiction of all bishops.

Nor. Then, that in all you writ to Rome, or else
To foreign princes, *Ego et Rex meus*
Was still inscrib'd; in which you brought the king
To be your servant.

Suf. Then, that without the knowledge
Either of king or council, when you went
Ambassador to the emperor, you made bold
To carry into Flanders the great seal.

Sur. Item, you sent a large commission
To Gregory de Cassado, to conclude,
Without the king's will or the state's allowance,
A league between his highness and Ferrara.

Suf. That, out of mere ambition, you have caus'd
Your holy hat to be stamp'd on the king's coin.

Sur. Then, that you have sent innumerable substance,—
By what means got, I leave to your own conscience,—
To furnish Rome, and to prepare the ways
You have for dignities; to the mere undoing
Of all the kingdom. Many more there are,
Which, since they are of you, and odious,
I will not taint my mouth with.

L. Ch. O my lord!
Press not a falling man too far; 'tis virtue:

308 objections: *accusations*
312 wrought: *contrived*
330 mere: *absolute*

311 First, that; *cf. n.*
321 Item: *likewise*

King Henry the Eighth, III. ii

His faults lie open to the laws; let them,
Not you, correct him. My heart weeps to see him 336
So little of his great self.
    Sur.   I forgive him.
    Suf. Lord Cardinal, the king's further pleasure is,
Because all those things you have done of late,
By your power legatine within this kingdom, 340
Fall into the compass of a *præmunire:*
That therefore such a writ be su'd against you,
To forfeit all your goods, lands, tenements,
Chattels, and whatsoever, and to be 344
Out of the king's protection. This is my charge.
    Nor. And so we'll leave you to your meditations
How to live better. For your stubborn answer
About the giving back the great seal to us, 348
The king shall know it, and, no doubt, shall thank you.
So fare you well, my little good Lord Cardinal.
                              Exeunt all but Wolsey.
    Car. So farewell to the little good you bear me.
Farewell! a long farewell, to all my greatness! 352
This is the state of man: to-day he puts forth
The tender leaves of hopes; to-morrow blossoms,
And bears his blushing honours thick upon him;
The third day comes a frost, a killing frost, 356
And when he thinks, good easy man, full surely
His greatness is a-ripening, nips his root,
And then he falls, as I do. I have ventur'd,
Like little wanton boys that swim on bladders, 360
This many summers in a sea of glory,
But far beyond my depth: my high-blown pride
At length broke under me, and now has left me,
Weary and old with service, to the mercy 364

---

341 præmunire: *the accusation of maintaining the papal power in England*   344 Chattels; *cf. n.*

Of a rude stream, that must for ever hide me.
Vain pomp and glory of this world, I hate ye.
I feel my heart now open'd. O how wretched
Is that poor man that hangs on princes' favours! 368
There is, betwixt that smile we would aspire to,
That sweet aspect of princes, and their ruin,
More pangs and fears than wars or women have;
And when he falls, he falls like Lucifer, 372
Never to hope again.

Enter Cromwell, standing amazed.

                    Why, how now, Cromwell!
  Crom. I have no power to speak, sir.
  Car.   What! amaz'd
At my misfortunes? Can thy spirit wonder
A great man should decline? Nay, an you weep, 376
I am fall'n indeed.
  Crom.   How does your Grace?
  Car.   Why, well:
Never so truly happy, my good Cromwell.
I know myself now; and I feel within me
A peace above all earthly dignities, 380
A still and quiet conscience. The king has cur'd me,
I humbly thank his Grace; and from these shoulders,
These ruin'd pillars, out of pity taken
A load would sink a navy, too much honour. 384
O, 'tis a burden, Cromwell, 'tis a burden
Too heavy for a man that hopes for heaven!
  Crom. I am glad your Grace has made that right use of it.
  Car. I hope I have: I am able now, methinks,— 388
Out of a fortitude of soul I feel,—
To endure more miseries and greater far

370 their ruin: *i.e. the ruin they cause*
372 Lucifer; *cf. n.*   376 an: *if*

King Henry the Eighth, III. ii

Than my weak-hearted enemies dare offer.
What news abroad?
   Crom.   The heaviest, and the worst, 392
Is your displeasure with the king.
   Car.   God bless him!
   Crom. The next is, that Sir Thomas More is chosen
Lord Chancellor in your place.
   Car.   That's somewhat sudden:
But he's a learned man. May he continue   396
Long in his highness' favour, and do justice
For truth's sake and his conscience; that his bones,
When he has run his course and sleeps in blessings,
May have a tomb of orphans' tears wept on him! 400
What more?
   Crom.   That Cranmer is return'd with welcome,
Install'd Lord Archbishop of Canterbury.
   Car. That's news indeed.
   Crom.   Last, that the Lady Anne,
Whom the king hath in secrecy long married,   404
This day was view'd in open as his queen,
Going to chapel; and the voice is now
Only about her coronation.
   Car. There was the weight that pull'd me down. O
      Cromwell!   408
The king has gone beyond me: all my glories
In that one woman I have lost for ever.
No sun shall ever usher forth mine honours,
Or gild again the noble troops that waited   412
Upon my smiles. Go, get thee from me, Cromwell;
I am a poor fall'n man, unworthy now
To be thy lord and master. Seek the king;—
That sun, I pray, may never set!—I have told him 416
What, and how true thou art: he will advance thee.

405 in open: *publicly*

Some little memory of me will stir him—
I know his noble nature—not to let
Thy hopeful service perish too. Good Cromwell, 420
Neglect him not; make use now, and provide
For thine own future safety.
   Crom.   O my lord!
Must I then leave you? must I needs forgo
So good, so noble, and so true a master? 424
Bear witness all that have not hearts of iron,
With what a sorrow Cromwell leaves his lord.
The king shall have my service; but my prayers
For ever and for ever shall be yours. 428
   Car. Cromwell, I did not think to shed a tear
In all my miseries: but thou hast forc'd me,
Out of thy honest truth, to play the woman.
Let's dry our eyes: and thus far hear me, Cromwell; 432
And when I am forgotten, as I shall be,
And sleep in dull cold marble, where no mention
Of me more must be heard of, say, I taught thee:
Say, Wolsey, that once trod the ways of glory, 436
And sounded all the depths and shoals of honour,
Found thee a way, out of his wrack, to rise in;
A sure and safe one, though thy master miss'd it.
Mark but my fall, and that that ruin'd me. 440
Cromwell, I charge thee, fling away ambition.
By that sin fell the angels: how can man then,
The image of his Maker, hope to win by it?
Love thyself last: cherish those hearts that hate thee;
Corruption wins not more than honesty.
Still in thy right hand carry gentle peace,
To silence envious tongues. Be just, and fear not:
Let all the ends thou aim'st at be thy country's, 448

King Henry the Eighth, IV. i

Thy God's, and truth's. Then if thou fall'st, O
    Cromwell,
Thou fall'st a blessed martyr. Serve the king;
And,—prithee, lead me in:
There take an inventory of all I have,   452
To the last penny: 'tis the king's. My robe,
And my integrity to heaven is all
I dare now call mine own. O Cromwell, Cromwell!
Had I but serv'd my God with half the zeal   456
I serv'd my king, he would not in mine age
Have left me naked to mine enemies.

  Crom. Good sir, have patience.
  Car.   So I have. Farewell
The hopes of court! my hopes in heaven do dwell. 460
                                      Exeunt.

ACT FOURTH

Scene One

[A Street in Westminster]

Enter two Gentlemen, meeting one another.

  1. Gent. Y' are well met once again.
  2. Gent.   So are you.
  1. Gent. You come to take your stand here, and behold
The Lady Anne pass from her coronation?
  2. Gent. 'Tis all my business. At our last encounter   4
The Duke of Buckingham came from his trial.
  1. Gent. 'Tis very true: but that time offer'd sorrow;
This, general joy.

450 Thou . . . martyr; *cf. n.*   456-458 *Cf. n.*
Scene One; *cf. n.*   4 last encounter; *cf. n.*

2. Gent.   'Tis well: the citizens,
I am sure, have shown at full their royal minds,
As, let 'em have their rights, they are ever forward,
In celebration of this day with shows,
Pageants, and sights of honour.
  1. Gent.   Never greater;
Nor, I'll assure you, better taken, sir.
  2. Gent. May I be bold to ask what that contains,
That paper in your hand?
  1. Gent.   Yes; 'tis the list
Of those that claim their offices this day
By custom of the coronation.
The Duke of Suffolk is the first, and claims
To be high-steward; next, the Duke of Norfolk,
He to be earl marshal: you may read the rest.
  2. Gent. I thank you, sir: had I not known those customs,
I should have been beholding to your paper.
But, I beseech you, what's become of Katharine,
The princess dowager? How goes her business?
  1. Gent. That I can tell you too. The Archbishop
Of Canterbury, accompanied with other
Learned and reverend fathers of his order,
Held a late court at Dunstable, six miles off
From Ampthill, where the princess lay; to which
She was often cited by them, but appear'd not:
And, to be short, for not appearance and
The king's late scruple, by the main assent
Of all these learned men she was divorc'd,
And the late marriage made of none effect:
Since which she was remov'd to Kimbolton,
Where she remains now sick.

15 Of those that claim; *cf. n.*   27 Dunstable; *cf. n.*
34 Kimbolton; *cf. n.*

King Henry the Eighth, IV. i

2. Gent.   Alas! good lady!   35
                             [*Trumpets.*]
The trumpets sound: stand close, the queen is coming.
                               Hautboys.

THE ORDER OF THE CORONATION.

1. *A lively flourish of trumpets.*
2. *Then, two Judges.*
3. Lord Chancellor, *with purse and mace before him.*
4. Choristers, *singing.*   *Music.*
5. Mayor of London, *bearing the mace. Then* Garter, *in his coat of arms, and on his head he wore a gilt copper crown.*
6. Marquess Dorset, *bearing a sceptre of gold, on his head a demi-coronal of gold. With him, the* Earl of Surrey, *bearing the rod of silver with the dove, crowned with an earl's coronet. Collars of Esses.*
7. Duke of Suffolk, *in his robe of estate, his coronet on his head, bearing a long white wand, as high-steward. With him, the* Duke of Norfolk, *with the rod of marshalship, a coronet on his head. Collars of Esses.*
8. *A canopy borne by four of the Cinque-ports; under it, the Queen in her robe; in her hair, richly adorned with pearl, crowned. On each side her, the* Bishops of London *and* Winchester.
9. *The old* Duchess of Norfolk, *in a coronal of gold, wrought with flowers, bearing the Queen's train.*
10. *Certain Ladies or Countesses, with plain circlets of gold, without flowers.*
       Exeunt, *first passing over the stage in order and state, and then, a great flourish of trumpets.*

36 S. d. The Order of the Coronation; *cf. n.*   Collars of Esses; *cf. n.*
in her hair: *with flowing hair*

2. Gent. A royal train, believe me. These I know;
Who's that that bears the sceptre?
1. Gent.   Marquess Dorset:
And that the Earl of Surrey with the rod.
2. Gent. A bold brave gentleman. That should be   40
The Duke of Suffolk?
1. Gent.   'Tis the same: high-steward.
2. Gent. And that my Lord of Norfolk?
1. Gent.   Yes.
2. Gent. [*Looking on the Queen.*] Heaven bless thee!
Thou hast the sweetest face I ever look'd on.
Sir, as I have a soul, she is an angel;   44
Our king has all the Indies in his arms,
And more and richer, when he strains that lady:
I cannot blame his conscience.
1. Gent.   They that bear
The cloth of honour over her, are four barons   48
Of the Cinque-ports.
2. Gent. Those men are happy; and so are all are near her.
I take it, she that carries up the train
Is that old noble lady, Duchess of Norfolk.   52
1. Gent. It is; and all the rest are countesses.
2. Gent. Their coronets say so. These are stars indeed;
And sometimes falling ones.
1. Gent.   No more of that.

Enter a third Gentleman.

God save you, sir! Where have you been broiling?   56
3. Gent. Among the crowd i' the Abbey; where a finger
Could not be wedg'd in more: I am stifled

King Henry the Eighth, IV. i

With the mere rankness of their joy.
 2. Gent.   You saw
The ceremony?
 3. Gent.   That I did.
 1. Gent.   How was it? 60
 3. Gent. Well worth the seeing.
 2. Gent.   Good sir, speak it to us.
 3. Gent. As well as I am able. The rich stream
Of lords and ladies, having brought the queen
To a prepar'd place in the choir, fell off 64
A distance from her; while her Grace sat down
To rest awhile, some half an hour or so,
In a rich chair of state, opposing freely
The beauty of her person to the people. 68
Believe me, sir, she is the goodliest woman
That ever lay by man: which when the people
Had the full view of, such a noise arose
As the shrouds make at sea in a stiff tempest, 72
As loud, and to as many tunes. Hats, cloaks,—
Doublets, I think,—flew up; and had their faces
Been loose, this day they had been lost. Such joy
I never saw before. Great-bellied women, 76
That had not half a week to go, like rams
In the old time of war, would shake the press,
And make 'em reel before 'em. No man living
Could say, 'This is my wife,' there; all were woven 80
So strangely in one piece.
 2. Gent.   But, what follow'd?
 3. Gent. At length her Grace rose, and with modest paces
Came to the altar; where she kneel'd, and, saintlike,
Cast her fair eyes to heaven and pray'd devoutly. 84

---

59 rankness: *exuberance*   62 ff. *Cf. n.*
67 opposing: *exposing*   72 shrouds: *sail-ropes*

Then rose again and bow'd her to the people:
When by the Archbishop of Canterbury
She had all the royal makings of a queen,
As holy oil, Edward Confessor's crown, 88
The rod, and bird of peace, and all such emblems
Laid nobly on her: which perform'd, the choir,
With all the choicest music of the kingdom,
Together sung *Te Deum*. So she parted, 92
And with the same full state pac'd back again
To York-place, where the feast is held.
  1. Gent.   Sir,
You must no more call it York-place, that's past;
For since the cardinal fell, that title's lost: 96
'Tis now the king's, and call'd Whitehall.
  3. Gent.   I know it;
But 'tis so lately alter'd that the old name
Is fresh about me.
  2. Gent.   What two reverend bishops
Were those that went on each side of the queen? 100
  3. Gent. Stokesly and Gardiner; the one of Winchester,—
Newly preferr'd from the king's secretary,—
The other, London.
  2. Gent.   He of Winchester
Is held no great good lover of the archbishop's, 104
The virtuous Cranmer.
  3. Gent.   All the land knows that:
However, yet there's no great breach; when it comes,
Cranmer will find a friend will not shrink from him.
  2. Gent. Who may that be, I pray you?
  3. Gent.   Thomas Cromwell: 108
A man in much esteem with the king, and truly

---

94 York-place; *cf. n.*   101 Stokesly and Gardiner; *cf. n.*
108 Thomas Cromwell; *cf. n.*

King Henry the Eighth, IV. ii

A worthy friend. The king
Has made him master o' the jewel house,
And one already of the privy-council. 112
  2. Gent. He will deserve more.
  3. Gent.   Yes, without all doubt.
Come, gentlemen, ye shall go my way, which
Is to the court, and there ye shall be my guests:
Something I can command. As I walk thither, 116
I'll tell ye more.
  Both.   You may command us, sir.
                                        Exeunt.

Scene Two

[*Kimbolton*]

Enter Katharine, Dowager, sick: led between Griffith her gentleman-usher and Patience her woman.

  Grif. How does your Grace?
  Kath.   O Griffith! sick to death!
My legs, like loaden branches, bow to the earth,
Willing to leave their burthen. Reach a chair:
So; now, methinks, I feel a little ease. 4
Didst thou not tell me, Griffith, as thou led'st me,
That the great child of honour, Cardinal Wolsey,
Was dead?
  Grif.   Yes, madam; but I think your Grace,
Out of the pain you suffer'd, gave no ear to 't. 8
  Kath. Prithee, good Griffith, tell me how he died:
If well, he stepp'd before me, happily,
For my example.

---

116 Something I can command: *I can order refreshments*
6, 7 Cardinal Wolsey, Was dead; *cf. n.*
9 tell me how he died; *cf. n.*   10 happily: *by good chance*

Grif.   Well, the voice goes, madam:
For after the stout Earl Northumberland   12
Arrested him at York, and brought him forward,
As a man sorely tainted, to his answer,
He fell sick suddenly, and grew so ill
He could not sit his mule.
Kath.   Alas! poor man.   16
Grif. At last, with easy roads, he came to Leicester;
Lodg'd in the abbey, where the reverend abbot,
With all his covent, honourably receiv'd him;
To whom he gave these words: 'O father abbot,   20
An old man, broken with the storms of state,
Is come to lay his weary bones among ye:
Give him a little earth for charity.'
So went to bed, where eagerly his sickness   24
Pursu'd him still; and three nights after this,
About the hour of eight,—which he himself
Foretold should be his last,—full of repentance,
Continual meditations, tears, and sorrows,   28
He gave his honours to the world again,
His blessed part to heaven, and slept in peace.

Kath. So may he rest; his faults lie gently on him!
Yet thus far, Griffith, give me leave to speak him,   32
And yet with charity. He was a man
Of an unbounded stomach, ever ranking
Himself with princes; one that by suggestion
Tied all the kingdom. Simony was fair-play.   36
His own opinion was his law; i' the presence
He would say untruths, and be ever double
Both in his words and meaning. He was never,

17 roads: *stages*   19 covent: *convent, body of monks*
31 So may he rest, etc.; *cf. n.*
32 speak him: *describe him; cf. II. iv. 164; III. i. 124*
34 stomach: *pride*
35, 36 by suggestion Tied: *by trickery restricted the liberties of*
36 Simony: *the selling of positions in the church*
37 i' the presence: *before the king*

But where he meant to ruin, pitiful. 40
His promises were, as he then was, mighty;
But his performance, as he is now, nothing:
Of his own body he was ill, and gave
The clergy ill example.

Grif.   Noble madam, 44
Men's evil manners live in brass; their virtues
We write in water. May it please your highness
To hear me speak his good now?

Kath.   Yes, good Griffith,
I were malicious else.

Grif.   This cardinal, 48
Though from an humble stock, undoubtedly
Was fashion'd to much honour. From his cradle
He was a scholar, and a ripe and good one:
Exceeding wise, fair-spoken, and persuading; 52
Lofty and sour to them that lov'd him not,
But to those men that sought him sweet as summer.
And though he were unsatisfied in getting,—
Which was a sin,—yet in bestowing, madam, 56
He was most princely. Ever witness for him
Those twins of learning that he rais'd in you,
Ipswich, and Oxford! one of which fell with him,
Unwilling to outlive the good that did it; 60
The other, though unfinish'd, yet so famous,
So excellent in art, and still so rising,
That Christendom shall ever speak his virtue.
His overthrow heap'd happiness upon him; 64
For then, and not till then, he felt himself,
And found the blessedness of being little.
And, to add greater honours to his age
Than man could give him, he died fearing God. 68

48 This cardinal; *cf. n.*   50 From his cradle; *cf. n.*
59 Ipswich, and Oxford; *cf. n.*   60 did: *i.e. founded*

Kath. After my death I wish no other herald,
No other speaker of my living actions,
To keep mine honour from corruption,
But such an honest chronicler as Griffith. 72
Whom I most hated living, thou hast made me,
With thy religious truth and modesty,
Now in his ashes honour. Peace be with him!
Patience, be near me still, and set me lower: 76
I have not long to trouble thee. Good Griffith,
Cause the musicians play me that sad note
I nam'd my knell, whilst I sit meditating
On that celestial harmony I go to. 80
Sad and solemn music.

Grif. She is asleep: good wench, let's sit down quiet,
For fear we wake her. Softly, gentle Patience.

The Vision.

Enter, solemnly tripping one after another, six Personages, clad in white robes, wearing on their heads garlands of bays, and golden vizards on their faces; branches of bays or palm in their hands. They first congee unto her, then dance; and, at certain changes, the first two hold a spare garland over her head; at which, the other four make reverend curtsies. Then, the two that held the garland deliver the same to the other next two, who observe the same order in their changes, and holding the garland over her head: which done, they deliver the same garland to the last two, who likewise observe the same order, at which,—as it were by inspiration,— she makes in her sleep signs of rejoicing, and holdeth up her hands to heaven: and so in their

82 S. d. congee: *bow*   changes: *movements of the dance*

dancing vanish, carrying the garland with them. The music continues.

Kath. Spirits of peace, where are ye? Are ye all gone,
And leave me here in wretchedness behind ye? 84
Grif. Madam, we are here.
Kath. It is not you I call for:
Saw ye none enter since I slept?
Grif. None, madam.
Kath. No? Saw you not even now a blessed troop
Invite me to a banquet; whose bright faces 88
Cast thousand beams upon me, like the sun?
They promis'd me eternal happiness,
And brought me garlands, Griffith, which I feel
I am not worthy yet to wear: I shall assuredly. 92
Grif. I am most joyful, madam, such good dreams
Possess your fancy.
Kath. Bid the music leave.
They are harsh and heavy to me. *Music ceases.*
Pat. Do you note
How much her Grace is alter'd on the sudden? 96
How long her face is drawn? How pale she looks,
And of an earthy cold? Mark her eyes!
Grif. She is going, wench. Pray, pray.
Pat. Heaven comfort her! 100

Enter a Messenger.

Mess. An't like your Grace,—
Kath. You are a saucy fellow:
Deserve we no more reverence?
Grif. You are to blame,
Knowing she will not lose her wonted greatness,
To use so rude behaviour; go to, kneel. 104

92 shall: *shall be worthy*　　94 music: *musicians*　　leave: *leave off*

Mess. I humbly do entreat your highness' pardon;
My haste made me unmannerly. There is staying
A gentleman, sent from the king, to see you.

Kath. Admit him entrance, Griffith: but this fellow
Let me ne'er see again. *Exit Messenger.*

Enter Lord Capucius.

If my sight fail not, 109
You should be lord ambassador from the emperor,
My royal nephew, and your name Capucius.

Cap. Madam, the same; your servant.

Kath. O, my lord, 112
The times and titles now are alter'd strangely
With me, since first you knew me. But, I pray you,
What is your pleasure with me?

Cap. Noble lady,
First, mine own service to your Grace; the next, 116
The king's request that I would visit you,
Who grieves much for your weakness, and by me
Sends you his princely commendations,
And heartily entreats you take good comfort. 120

Kath. O, my good lord, that comfort comes too late!
'Tis like a pardon after execution:
That gentle physic, given in time, had cur'd me;
But now I am past all comforts here but prayers. 124
How does his highness?

Cap. Madam, in good health.

Kath. So may he ever do, and ever flourish,
When I shall dwell with worms, and my poor name
Banish'd the kingdom. Patience, is that letter 128
I caus'd you write, yet sent away?

Pat. No, madam.
[*Giving it to Katharine.*]

111 Capucius; *cf. n.*

Kath. Sir, I most humbly pray you to deliver
This to my lord the king.
Cap. Most willing, madam. 131
Kath. In which I have commended to his goodness
The model of our chaste loves, his young daughter:
The dews of heaven fall thick in blessings on her!
Beseeching him to give her virtuous breeding,—
She is young, and of a noble modest nature, 136
I hope she will deserve well,—and a little
To love her for her mother's sake, that lov'd him,
Heaven knows how dearly. My next poor petition
Is, that his noble Grace would have some pity 140
Upon my wretched women, that so long
Have follow'd both my fortunes faithfully:
Of which there is not one, I dare avow,—
And now I should not lie,—but will deserve, 144
For virtue, and true beauty of the soul,
For honesty and decent carriage,
A right good husband, let him be a noble;
And, sure, those men are happy that shall have 'em. 148
The last is, for my men: they are the poorest,
But poverty could never draw 'em from me;
That they may have their wages duly paid 'em,
And something over to remember me by. 152
If heaven had pleas'd to have given me longer life
And able means, we had not parted thus.
These are the whole contents: and, good my lord,
By that you love the dearest in this world, 156
As you wish Christian peace to souls departed,
Stand these poor people's friend, and urge the king
To do me this last right.
Cap. By heaven, I will,

133 model: *memorial*   his young daughter: *Mary Tudor*
142 both my fortunes: *prosperity and adversity*

Or let me lose the fashion of a man! 160
  Kath. I thank you, honest lord. Remember me
In all humility unto his highness:
Say his long trouble now is passing 163
Out of this world. Tell him, in death I bless'd him,
For so I will. Mine eyes grow dim. Farewell,
My lord. Griffith, farewell. Nay, Patience,
You must not leave me yet. I must to bed; 167
Call in more women. When I am dead, good wench,
Let me be us'd with honour: strew me over
With maiden flowers, that all the world may know
I was a chaste wife to my grave. Embalm me,
Then lay me forth: although unqueen'd, yet like 172
A queen, and daughter to a king, inter me.
I can no more.   *Exeunt, leading Katharine.*

ACT FIFTH

Scene One

[*London. A Gallery in the Palace*]

Enter Gardiner, Bishop of Winchester, a Page with a torch before him, met by Sir Thomas Lovell.

  Gar. It's one o'clock, boy, is 't not?
  Boy.   It hath struck.
  Gar. These should be hours for necessities,
Not for delights: times to repair our nature
With comforting repose, and not for us 4
To waste these times. Good hour of night, Sir Thomas!
Whither so late?

---

160 fashion: *shape*   Act Fifth; *cf. n.*

King Henry the Eighth, V.i

Lov.   Came you from the king, my lord?
Gar. I did, Sir Thomas; and left him at primero
With the Duke of Suffolk.
Lov.   I must to him too,   8
Before he go to bed. I'll take my leave.
Gar. Not yet, Sir Thomas Lovell. What's the matter?
It seems you are in haste: and if there be
No great offence belongs to 't, give your friend   12
Some touch of your late business. Affairs, that walk—
As they say spirits do—at midnight, have
In them a wilder nature than the business
That seeks dispatch by day.
Lov.   My lord, I love you,   16
And durst commend a secret to your ear
Much weightier than this work. The queen's in labour,
They say, in great extremity; and fear'd
She'll with the labour end.
Gar.   The fruit she goes with 20
I pray for heartily, that it may find
Good time, and live: but for the stock, Sir Thomas,
I wish it grubb'd up now.
Lov.   Methinks I could
Cry the amen; and yet my conscience says   24
She's a good creature, and, sweet lady, does
Deserve our better wishes.
Gar.   But, sir, sir,
Hear me, Sir Thomas: y' are a gentleman
Of mine own way. I know you wise, religious;   28
And, let me tell you, it will ne'er be well,
'Twill not, Sir Thomas Lovell, take 't of me,
Till Cranmer, Cromwell, her two hands, and she,

---

7 primero: *a game of cards*   13 touch: *hint*   late: *i.e. nocturnal*
19 fear'd: *it is feared*   28 way: *way of thinking*

Sleep in their graves.
 Lov.   Now, sir, you speak of two 32
The most remark'd i' the kingdom. As for Cromwell,
Beside that of the jewel-house, is made master
O' the rolls, and the king's secretary; further, sir,
Stands in the gap and trade of moe preferments, 36
With which the time will load him. Th' archbishop
Is the king's hand and tongue; and who dare speak
One syllable against him?
 Gar.   Yes, yes, Sir Thomas,
There are that dare; and I myself have ventur'd 40
To speak my mind of him: and indeed this day,
—Sir, I may tell it you,—I think I have
Incens'd the lords o' the council that he is—
For so I know he is, they know he is— 44
A most arch heretic, a pestilence
That does infect the land: with which they mov'd
Have broken with the king, who hath so far
Given ear to our complaint,—of his great grace 48
And princely care, foreseeing those fell mischiefs
Our reasons laid before him,—hath commanded
To-morrow morning to the council-board
He be convented. He's a rank weed, Sir Thomas, 52
And we must root him out. From your affairs
I hinder you too long: good-night, Sir Thomas!
 Lov. Many good-nights, my lord. I rest your serv-
  ant.   *Exeunt Gardiner and Page.*

Enter King and Suffolk.

 King. Charles, I will play no more to-night; 56
My mind's not on 't; you are too hard for me.

34 that: *the mastership; cf. IV. i. 111*   is: *he is*
36 gap and trade: *the opening and track by which preferments come*
43 Incens'd: *impressed upon*
46 with which they mov'd: *moved by which they*
47 broken with: *communicated with*   52 convented: *summoned*

King Henry the Eighth, V. i

Suf. Sir, I did never win of you before.
King. But little, Charles;
Nor shall not when my fancy's on my play. 60
Now, Lovell, from the queen what is the news?
Lov. I could not personally deliver to her
What you commanded me, but by her woman
I sent your message; who return'd her thanks 64
In the great'st humbleness, and desir'd your highness
Most heartily to pray for her.
    King.   What sayst thou? Ha?
To pray for her? what, is she crying out?
    Lov. So said her woman; and that her sufferance made 68
Almost each pang a death.
    King.   Alas! good lady.
    Suf. God safely quit her of her burthen, and
With gentle travail, to the gladding of
Your highness with an heir!
    King.   'Tis midnight, Charles; 72
Prithee, to bed; and in thy prayers remember
Th' estate of my poor queen. Leave me alone;
For I must think of that which company
Would not be friendly to.
    Suf.   I wish your highness 76
A quiet night, and my good mistress will
Remember in my prayers.
    King.   Charles, good-night.
                          Exit Suffolk.

Enter Sir Anthony Denny.

Well, sir, what follows?
    Den. Sir, I have brought my lord the archbishop, 80
As you commanded me.

74 estate: *condition*

King.   Ha! Canterbury?
Den. Ay, my good lord.
King.   'Tis true: where is he, Denny?
Den. He attends your highness' pleasure.
King.   Bring him to us.
                                  [*Exit Denny.*]
    Lov. [*Aside.*] This is about that which the bishop
       spake: 84
I am happily come hither.

              Enter Cranmer and Denny.

King.   Avoid the gallery.
                           Lovell seems to stay.
Ha! I have said. Begone.
What!—   *Exeunt Lovell and Denny.*
    Cran. I am fearful. Wherefore frowns he thus? 88
'Tis his aspect of terror. All's not well.
    King. How now, my lord! You do desire to know
Wherefore I sent for you.
    Cran.   [*Kneeling.*] It is my duty
T' attend your highness' pleasure.
    King.   Pray you, arise, 92
My good and gracious Lord of Canterbury.
Come, you and I must walk a turn together:
I have news to tell you. Come, come, give me your
      hand.
Ah! my good lord, I grieve at what I speak,   96
And am right sorry to repeat what follows.
I have, and most unwillingly, of late
Heard many grievous, I do say, my lord,
Grievous complaints of you; which, being consider'd,
Have mov'd us and our council, that you shall
This morning come before us; where, I know,

85 happily: *fortunately*   Avoid: *go out from*

King Henry the Eighth, V. i

You cannot with such freedom purge yourself,
But that, till further trial in those charges 104
Which will require your answer, you must take
Your patience to you, and be well contented
To make your house our Tower: you, a brother of us,
It fits we thus proceed, or else no witness 108
Would come against you.

Cran. [*Kneeling.*] I humbly thank your highness;
And am right glad to catch this good occasion
Most thoroughly to be winnow'd, where my chaff
And corn shall fly asunder; for I know 112
There's none stands under more calumnious tongues
Than I myself, poor man.

King. Stand up, good Canterbury:
Thy truth and thy integrity is rooted
In us, thy friend. Give me thy hand, stand up: 116
Prithee, let's walk. Now, by my holidame,
What manner of man are you? My lord, I look'd
You would have given me your petition, that
I should have ta'en some pains to bring together 120
Yourself and your accusers; and to have heard you,
Without indurance, further.

Cran. Most dread liege,
The good I stand on is my truth and honesty:
If they shall fail, I, with mine enemies, 124
Will triumph o'er my person, which I weigh not,
Being of those virtues vacant. I fear nothing
What can be said against me.

King. Know you not
How your state stands i' the world, with the whole world? 128

107 you . . . us: *since you are of nearly royal rank (as head of the church)* 117 holidame: *halidom, a customary oath*
122 indurance: *imprisonment*   123 The good I stand on: *my defense*
125 my person . . . weigh not: *my body which I do not value*
126 Being: *if it be*   nothing. *not at all*

Your enemies are many, and not small; their practices
Must bear the same proportion; and not ever
The justice and the truth o' the question carries
The due o' the verdict with it. At what ease 132
Might corrupt minds procure knaves as corrupt
To swear against you? Such things have been done.
You are potently oppos'd, and with a malice
Of as great size. Ween you of better luck, 136
I mean in perjur'd witness, than your Master,
Whose minister you are, whiles here he liv'd
Upon this naughty earth? Go to, go to;
You take a precipice for no leap of danger, 140
And woo your own destruction.
   Cran.   God and your majesty
Protect mine innocence! or I fall into
The trap is laid for me!
   King.   Be of good cheer;
They shall no more prevail than we give way to. 144
Keep comfort to you; and this morning see
You do appear before them. If they shall chance,
In charging you with matters, to commit you,
The best persuasions to the contrary 148
Fail not to use, and with what vehemency
Th' occasion shall instruct you. If entreaties
Will render you no remedy, this ring
Deliver them, and your appeal to us 152
There make before them. Look! the good man weeps:
He's honest, on mine honour. God's blest mother!
I swear he is true-hearted; and a soul
None better in my kingdom. Get you gone, 156

---

129 practices: *plots*
130 bear . . . proportion: *likewise be many and not small*
    ever: *in every case*   136 Ween: *dream*
143 is: *which is*

King Henry the Eighth, V.i

And do as I have bid you. *Exit Cranmer.*
       He has strangled
His language in his tears.

Enter Old Lady.

Gent. within. Come back: what mean you? 159
 Lady. I'll not come back; the tidings that I bring
Will make my boldness manners. Now, good angels
Fly o'er thy royal head, and shade thy person
Under their blessed wings!
 King.   Now, by thy looks
I guess thy message. Is the queen deliver'd? 164
Say, ay; and of a boy.
 Lady.   Ay, ay, my liege;
And of a lovely boy: the God of heaven
Both now and ever bless her! 'Tis a girl,
Promises boys hereafter. Sir, your queen 168
Desires your visitation, and to be
Acquainted with this stranger: 'tis as like you
As cherry is to cherry.
 King.   Lovell!

[*Enter Lovell.*]

 Lov.   Sir! 171
 King. Give her an hundred marks. I'll to the
  queen.   *Exit King.*
 Lady. An hundred marks! By this light, I'll ha'
  more.
An ordinary groom is for such payment.
I will have more, or scold it out of him.
Said I for this, the girl was like to him? 176
I will have more, or else unsay't; and now,
While it is hot, I'll put it to the issue.
       Exit Lady [*with Lovell*].

Scene Two

[*The Lobby before the Council-Chamber*]

Enter Cranmer, Archbishop of Canterbury.

Cran. I hope I am not too late; and yet the gentleman,
That was sent to me from the council, pray'd me
To make great haste. All fast? what means this? Ho!
Who waits there?

Enter Keeper.

Sure, you know me?
Keep. Yes, my lord; 4
But yet I cannot help you.
Cran. Why?
Keep. Your Grace must wait till you be call'd for.

Enter Doctor Butts.

Cran. So.
Butts. [*Aside.*] This is a piece of malice. I am glad
I came this way so happily. The king 8
Shall understand it presently.
Cran. [*Aside.*] 'Tis Butts,
The king's physician. As he pass'd along,
How earnestly he cast his eyes upon me.
Pray heaven he sound not my disgrace! For certain, 12
This is of purpose laid by some that hate me,—
God turn their hearts! I never sought their malice,—
To quench mine honour: they would shame to make me
Wait else at door, a fellow-counsellor 16
'Mong boys, grooms, and lackeys. But their pleasures

---

12 sound: *penetrate, discover*

King Henry the Eighth, V. iii

Must be fulfill'd, and I attend with patience.

Enter the King and Butts at a window above.

Butts. I'll show your Grace the strangest sight,—
King.   What's that, Butts?
Butts. I think your highness saw this many a day. 20
King. Body o' me, where is it?
Butts.   There, my lord:
The high promotion of his Grace of Canterbury,
Who holds his state at door 'mongst pursuivants,
Pages, and footboys.
King.   Ha! 'Tis he, indeed.   24
Is this the honour they do one another?
'Tis well there's one above 'em yet. I had thought
They had parted so much honesty among 'em,—
At least, good manners,—as not thus to suffer   28
A man of his place, and so near our favour,
To dance attendance on their lordships' pleasures,
And at the door too, like a post with packets.
By holy Mary, Butts, there's knavery: 32
Let 'em alone, and draw the curtain close;
We shall hear more anon.   [*Exeunt above.*]

Scene Three

[*The Council-Chamber*]

A council-table brought in with chairs and stoves, and placed under the state. Enter Lord Chancellor, places himself at the upper end of the table on the left hand; a seat being left void above him, as for Canterbury's seat; Duke of Suffolk, Duke of Nor-

18 S. d. at a window above; *cf. n.*
23 pursuivants: *minor officers attendant upon heralds*
27 parted: *divided*
31 post with packets: *a messenger with letters*

folk, Surrey, Lord Chamberlain, Gardiner seat themselves in order on each side; Cromwell at lower end as Secretary.

Chan. Speak to the business, Master Secretary:
Why are we met in council?
Crom. Please your honours,
The chief cause concerns his Grace of Canterbury.
Gar. Has he had knowledge of it?
Crom. Yes.
Nor. Who waits there? 4
Keep. Without, my noble lords?
Gar. Yes.
Keep. My lord archbishop:
And has done half an hour, to know your pleasures.
Chan. Let him come in.
Keep. Your Grace may enter now.
Cranmer approaches the council-table.
Chan. My good lord archbishop, I'm very sorry 8
To sit here at this present and behold
That chair stand empty: but we all are men,
In our own natures frail, and capable
Of our flesh; few are angels: out of which frailty 12
And want of wisdom, you, that best should teach us,
Have misdemean'd yourself, and not a little:
Toward the king first, then his laws, in filling
The whole realm, by your teaching and your chaplains,— 16
For so we are inform'd,—with new opinions,
Divers and dangerous, which are heresies,
And, not reform'd, may prove pernicious.
Gar. Which reformation must be sudden too, 20
My noble lords; for those that tame wild horses

11, 12 capable . . . flesh: *susceptible of being influenced by our fleshly nature* 19 not: *if not*

Pace 'em not in their hands to make 'em gentle,
But stop their mouths with stubborn bits, and spur
   'em,
Till they obey the manage. If we suffer—　　　24
Out of our easiness and childish pity
To one man's honour—this contagious sickness,
Farewell all physic: and what follows then?
Commotions, uproars, with a general taint　　　28
Of the whole state: as, of late days, our neighbours,
The upper Germany, can dearly witness,
Yet freshly pitied in our memories.
　Cran. My good lords, hitherto in all the progress 32
Both of my life and office, I have labour'd,
And with no little study, that my teaching
And the strong course of my authority
Might go one way, and safely; and the end　　　36
Was ever, to do well: nor is there living,—
I speak it with a single heart, my lords,—
A man that more detests, more stirs against,
Both in his private conscience and his place,　　　40
Defacers of a public peace, than I do.
Pray heaven the king may never find a heart
With less allegiance in it! Men that make
Envy and crooked malice nourishment　　　44
Dare bite the best. I do beseech your lordships
That, in this case of justice, my accusers,
Be what they will, may stand forth face to face,
And freely urge against me.
　Suf.　　　　　　　Nay, my lord,　　　48
That cannot be: you are a counsellor,
And by that virtue no man dare accuse you.
　Gar. My lord, because we have business of more
   moment,

24 manage: *rider's control*　　　　29-31 as, of late days, etc.; *cf. n.*

We will be short with you. 'Tis his highness'
    pleasure,
And our consent, for better trial of you,
From hence you be committed to the Tower;
Where, being but a private man again,
You shall know many dare accuse you boldly,
More than, I fear, you are provided for.
   Cran. Ah, my good Lord of Winchester, I thank
you!
You are always my good friend: if your will pass,
I shall both find your lordship judge and juror,
You are so merciful. I see your end;
'Tis my undoing. Love and meekness, lord,
Become a churchman better than ambition:
Win straying souls with modesty again,
Cast none away. That I shall clear myself,
Lay all the weight ye can upon my patience,
I make as little doubt as you do conscience
In doing daily wrongs. I could say more,
But reverence to your calling makes me modest.
   Gar. My lord, my lord, you are a sectary;
That's the plain truth: your painted gloss discovers,
To men that understand you, words and weakness.
   Crom. My Lord of Winchester, y' are a little,
By your good favour, too sharp; men so noble,
However faulty, yet should find respect
For what they have been: 'tis a cruelty
To load a falling man.
   Gar.   Good Master Secretary,
I cry your honour mercy; you may worst
Of all this table say so.

---

65 Lay: *though you lay*   69 modest: *moderate*
70 sectary: *a member of a religious sect, therefore hostile to the Church*   71 discovers: *reveals*
72 words and weakness: *weak verbosity*

Crom.   Why, my lord?
Gar. Do not I know you for a favourer   80
Of this new sect? ye are not sound.
    Crom.   Not sound?
    Gar. Not sound, I say.
    Crom.   Would you were half so honest!
Men's prayers then would seek you, not their fears.
    Gar. I shall remember this bold language.
    Crom.   Do.   84
Remember your bold life too.
    Chan.   This is too much;
Forbear, for shame, my lords.
    Gar.   I have done.
    Crom.   And I.
    Chan. Then thus for you, my lord: it stands agreed,
I take it, by all voices, that forthwith   88
You be convey'd to the Tower a prisoner;
There to remain till the king's further pleasure
Be known unto us. Are you all agreed, lords?
    All. We are.
    Cran.   Is there no other way of mercy,   92
But I must needs to the Tower, my lords?
    Gar.   What other
Would you expect? You are strangely troublesome.
Let some o' the guard be ready there.

                Enter the Guard.

    Cran.   For me?
Must I go like a traitor thither?
    Gar.   Receive him,   96
And see him safe i' the Tower.
    Cran.   Stay, good my lords;
I have a little yet to say. Look there, my lords;

---

85 This is too much; *cf. n.*

By virtue of that ring I take my cause
Out of the gripes of cruel men, and give it 100
To a most noble judge, the king my master.

   Chan. This is the king's ring.
   Sur.   'Tis no counterfeit?
   Suf. 'Tis the right ring, by heaven! I told ye all,
When we first put this dangerous stone a-rolling, 104
'Twould fall upon ourselves.
   Nor.   Do you think, my lords,
The king will suffer but the little finger
Of this man to be vex'd?
   Chan.   'Tis now too certain:
How much more is his life in value with him? 108
Would I were fairly out on 't.
   Crom.   My mind gave me,
In seeking tales and informations
Against this man—whose honesty the devil
And his disciples only envy at— 112
Ye blew the fire that burns ye: now have at ye!

   Enter King, frowning on them: takes his seat.

   Gar. Dread sovereign, how much are we bound to heaven
In daily thanks, that gave us such a prince,
Not only good and wise, but most religious: 116
One that in all obedience makes the Church
The chief aim of his honour; and to strengthen
That holy duty, out of dear respect,
His royal self in judgment comes to hear 120
The cause betwixt her and this great offender.
   King. You were ever good at sudden commendations,
Bishop of Winchester; but know, I come not

---

103 right: *genuine*   109 My mind gave me: *I suspected*

King Henry the Eighth, V. iii

To hear such flattery now, and in my presence 124
They are too thin and base to hide offences.
To me you cannot reach; you play the spaniel,
And think with wagging of your tongue to win me;
But, whatsoe'er thou tak'st me for, I'm sure 128
Thou hast a cruel nature and a bloody.
[*To Cranmer.*] Good man, sit down. Now let me see the proudest
He, that dares most, but wag his finger at thee.
By all that's holy, he had better starve 132
Than but once think his place becomes thee not.

  Sur. May it please your Grace,—
  King.   No, sir, it does not please me.
I had thought I had had men of some understanding
And wisdom of my council; but I find none. 136
Was it discretion, lords, to let this man,
This good man,—few of you deserve that title,—
This honest man, wait like a lousy footboy
At chamber-door? and one as great as you are? 140
Why, what a shame was this! Did my commission
Bid ye so far forget yourselves? I gave ye
Power as he was a counsellor to try him,
Not as a groom. There's some of ye, I see, 144
More out of malice than integrity,
Would try him to the utmost, had ye mean;
Which ye shall never have while I live.

  Chan.   Thus far,
My most dread sovereign, may it like your Grace 148
To let my tongue excuse all. What was purpos'd
Concerning his imprisonment was rather—
If there be faith in men—meant for his trial
And fair purgation to the world, than malice,— 152

---

133 his place; *cf. n.*   136 of: *as members of*
146 mean: *opportunity*

I'm sure, in me.
 King.   Well, well, my lords, respect him;
Take him, and use him well; he's worthy of it.
I will say thus much for him: if a prince
May be beholding to a subject, I   156
Am, for his love and service, so to him.
Make me no more ado, but all embrace him:
Be friends, for shame, my lords! My Lord of Canterbury,
I have a suit which you must not deny me;   160
That is, a fair young maid that yet wants baptism:
You must be godfather, and answer for her.
 Cran. The greatest monarch now alive may glory
In such an honour: how may I deserve it,   164
That am a poor and humble subject to you?
  King. Come, come, my lord, you'd spare
  your spoons. You shall have two noble partners
  with you: the old Duchess of Norfolk, and Lady 168
Marquess Dorset. Will these please you?
Once more, my Lord of Winchester, I charge you,
Embrace and love this man.
 Gar.   With a true heart
And brother-love I do it.
 Cran.   And let heaven   172
Witness, how dear I hold this confirmation.
 King. Good man! those joyful tears show thy true heart.
The common voice, I see, is verified
Of thee, which says thus: 'Do my Lord of Canterbury   176
A shrewd turn, and he's your friend for ever.'
Come, lords, we trifle time away: I long

166 spare your spoons: *save christening presents*
173 confirmation: *assurance*
177 shrewd: *malicious (i.e. he returns good for evil)*

King Henry the Eighth, V. iv 111

To have this young one made a Christian.
As I have made ye one, lords, one remain; 180
So I grow stronger, you more honour gain.   *Exeunt.*

Scene Four

[*The Palace-Yard*]

Noise and tumult within.   Enter Porter and his Man.

Port. You'll leave your noise anon, ye rascals.
Do you take the court for Parish-garden? ye rude
slaves, leave your gaping.

[*Voice*] *Within.* Good Master Porter, I belong 4
to the larder.

Port. Belong to the gallows, and be hanged,
ye rogue! Is this a place to roar in? Fetch
me a dozen crab-tree staves, and strong ones: 8
these are but switches to 'em. I'll scratch your
heads: you must be seeing christenings! Do
you look for ale and cakes here, you rude
rascals? 12

Man. Pray, sir, be patient: 'tis as much impossible—
Unless we sweep 'em from the doors with cannons—
To scatter 'em, as 'tis to make 'em sleep
On May-day morning; which will never be. 16
We may as well push against Paul's as stir 'em.

Port. How got they in, and be hang'd?

Man. Alas, I know not; how gets the tide in?
As much as one sound cudgel of four foot— 20
You see the poor remainder—could distribute,
I made no spare, sir.

Port.   You did nothing, sir.

---
2 Parish-garden; *cf. n.*
5 larder: *the pantry (therefore he had the right to enter)*
16 May-day morning; *cf. n.*   17 Paul's: *St. Paul's Cathedral*

Man. I am not Samson, nor Sir Guy, nor Colbrand,
To mow 'em down before me; but if I spar'd any   24
That had a head to hit, either young or old,
He or she, cuckold or cuckold-maker,
Let me ne'er hope to see a chine again;
And that I would not for a cow, God save her!   28

Within. Do you hear, Master Porter?

Port. I shall be with you presently, good Master puppy. Keep the door close, sirrah.

Man. What would you have me do?   32

Port. What should you do, but knock 'em down by the dozens? Is this Moorfields to muster in? or have we some strange Indian with the great tool come to court, the women so   36
besiege us? Bless me, what a fry of fornication is at door! On my Christian conscience, this one christening will beget a thousand: here will be father, godfather, and all together.   40

Man. The spoons will be the bigger, sir. There is a fellow somewhat near the door, he should be a brazier by his face, for, o' my conscience, twenty of the dog days now reign in's nose: all   44
that stand about him are under the line, they need no other penance. That fire-drake did I hit three times on the head, and three times was his nose discharged against me: he stands there,   48
like a mortar-piece, to blow us. There was a haberdasher's wife of small wit near him, that railed upon me till her pinked porringer fell off

---

23 *Cf. n.*
28 for a cow; *cf. n.*
27 chine: *roast of beef*
34 Moorfields; *cf. n.*
35 strange Indian; *cf. n.*
41 The spoons; *cf. n.*
43 brazier: *worker in brass*
45 under the line: *under the equator (where it is hot)*
46 fire-drake: *fiery dragon (the man with the red nose)*
49 mortar-piece: *small cannon*
51 pinked porringer: *a bowl-shaped hat slashed with holes*

King Henry the Eighth, V. iv

her head, for kindling such a combustion in the 52
state. I missed the meteor once, and hit that
woman, who cried out, 'Clubs!' when I might
see from far some forty truncheoners draw to
her succour, which were the hope o' the Strand, 56
where she was quartered. They fell on; I made
good my place; at length they came to the
broomstaff to me; I defied 'em still; when
suddenly a file of boys behind 'em, loose shot, 60
delivered such a shower of pebbles, that I was
fain to draw mine honour in, and let 'em win
the work. The devil was amongst 'em, I think,
surely. 64

Port. These are the youths that thunder at a
playhouse, and fight for bitten apples; that no
audience, but the Tribulation of Tower-hill, or
the Limbs of Limehouse, their dear brothers, are 68
able to endure. I have some of 'em in *Limbo
Patrum,* and there they are like to dance these
three days; besides the running banquet of two
beadles, that is to come. 72

Enter Lord Chamberlain.

L. Ch. Mercy o' me, what a multitude are here!
They grow still too, from all parts they are coming,
As if we kept a fair here! Where are these porters,
These lazy knaves? Y' have made a fine hand, fel-
   lows: 76
There's a trim rabble let in. Are all these
Your faithful friends o' the suburbs? We shall have
Great store of room, no doubt, left for the ladies,
When they pass back from the christening.

---

54 Clubs; *cf. n.*　　56 Strand: *street in London*　　63 work: *outwork*
67, 68 Tribulation . . . Limehouse; *cf. n.*　　69 Limbo Patrum: *i.e. jail*
71 running banquet; *cf. n.*　　76 fine hand: *pretty business*

Port.   An 't please your honour, 80
We are but men; and what so many may do,
Not being torn a-pieces, we have done:
An army cannot rule 'em.
   L. Ch.   As I live,
If the king blame me for 't, I'll lay ye all   84
By th' heels, and suddenly; and on your heads
Clap round fines for neglect: y' are lazy knaves;
And here ye lie baiting of bombards, when
Ye should do service. Hark! the trumpets sound; 88
They're come already from the christening.
Go, break among the press, and find a way out
To let the troop pass fairly, or I'll find
A Marshalsea shall hold ye play these two months. 92
   Port. Make way there for the princess.
   Man.   You great fellow,
Stand close up, or I'll make your head ache.
   Port. You i' the camlet, get up o' the rail:
I'll pick you o'er the pales else.   *Exeunt.*

Scene Five

[*The Palace*]

Enter trumpets, sounding; then two Aldermen, Lord Mayor, Garter, Cranmer, Duke of Norfolk, with his marshal's staff, Duke of Suffolk, two Noblemen bearing great standing-bowls for the christening gifts: then four Noblemen bearing a canopy, under which the Duchess of Norfolk, godmother,

---

81, 82 what . . . a-pieces: *what our number may do without being torn to pieces*   86 round: *heavy*
87 baiting of bombards: *drinking deep*
92 Marshalsea: *a prison*   95 i' the camlet: *in the woolen suit*
96 pick: *pitch*   pales: *palisade*   Scene Five; *cf. n.*
S. d. Garter: *the chief herald*

*bearing the child, richly habited in a mantle, &c.,
train borne by a Lady: then follows the Marchioness Dorset, the other godmother, and ladies.
The troop pass once about the stage, and Garter
speaks.*

Gart. Heaven, from thy endless goodness,
send prosperous life, long, and ever happy, to
the high and mighty Princess of England, Elizabeth! 4

Flourish. Enter King and Guard.

Cran. [*Kneeling.*] And to your royal Grace, and the
good queen,
My noble partners and myself thus pray:
All comfort, joy, in this most gracious lady,
Heaven ever laid up to make parents happy, 8
May hourly fall upon ye!
King. Thank you, good lord archbishop:
What is her name?
Cran. Elizabeth.
King. Stand up, lord.
[*The King kisses the Child.*]
With this kiss take my blessing; God protect thee!
Into whose hand I give thy life.
Cran. Amen. 12
King. My noble gossips, y' have been too prodigal:
I thank ye heartily: so shall this lady
When she has so much English.
Cran. Let me speak, sir,
For heaven now bids me; and the words I utter 16
Let none think flattery, for they'll find 'em truth.
This royal infant,—heaven still move about her!—
Though in her cradle, yet now promises

6 My noble partners: *the other sponsors*   13 prodigal: *generous*

Upon this land a thousand thousand blessings, 20
Which time shall bring to ripeness. She shall be—
But few now living can behold that goodness—
A pattern to all princes living with her,
And all that shall succeed: Saba was never 24
More covetous of wisdom and fair virtue
Than this pure soul shall be: all princely graces,
That mould up such a mighty piece as this is,
With all the virtues that attend the good, 28
Shall still be doubled on her; truth shall nurse her;
Holy and heavenly thoughts still counsel her;
She shall be lov'd and fear'd. Her own shall bless her;
Her foes shake like a field of beaten corn, 32
And hang their heads with sorrow. Good grows with her.
In her days every man shall eat in safety
Under his own vine what he plants; and sing
The merry songs of peace to all his neighbours. 36
God shall be truly known; and those about her
From her shall read the perfect ways of honour,
And by those claim their greatness, not by blood.
Nor shall this peace sleep with her; but as when 40
The bird of wonder dies, the maiden phœnix,
Her ashes new-create another heir
As great in admiration as herself,
So shall she leave her blessedness to one,— 44
When heaven shall call her from this cloud of darkness,—
Who, from the sacred ashes of her honour,
Shall star-like rise, as great in fame as she was,

24 Saba: *the Queen of Sheba*
43 great in admiration: *admirable*
44 to one: *James I, the successor of Elizabeth*

King Henry the Eighth, V. v

And so stand fix'd. Peace, plenty, love, truth, terror, 48
That were the servants to this chosen infant,
Shall then be his, and like a vine grow to him:
Wherever the bright sun of heaven shall shine,
His honour and the greatness of his name 52
Shall be, and make new nations. He shall flourish,
And, like a mountain cedar, reach his branches
To all the plains about him. Our children's children
Shall see this, and bless heaven.
  King.   Thou speakest wonders. 56
  Cran. She shall be, to the happiness of England,
An aged princess; many days shall see her,
And yet no day without a deed to crown it.
Would I had known no more! but she must die, 60
She must, the saints must have her; yet a virgin,
A most unspotted lily shall she pass
To the ground, and all the world shall mourn her.
  King. O lord archbishop! 64
Thou hast made me now a man: never, before
This happy child, did I get anything.
This oracle of comfort has so pleas'd me,
That when I am in heaven, I shall desire 68
To see what this child does, and praise my Maker.
I thank ye all. To you, my good Lord Mayor,
And your good brethren, I am much beholding;
I have receiv'd much honour by your presence, 72
And ye shall find me thankful. Lead the way, lords:
Ye must all see the queen, and she must thank ye;
She will be sick else. This day, no man think
H'as business at his house; for all shall stay: 76
This little one shall make it holiday.   *Exeunt.*

THE EPILOGUE.

'Tis ten to one, this play can never please
All that are here. Some come to take their ease
And sleep an act or two; but those, we fear,
We've frighted with our trumpets; so, 'tis clear 4
They'll say 'tis naught: others, to hear the city
Abus'd extremely, and to cry, 'That's witty!'
Which we have not done neither: that, I fear,
All the expected good we're like to hear 8
For this play at this time is only in
The merciful construction of good women;
For such a one we show'd 'em: if they smile,
And say 'twill do, I know within a while 12
All the best men are ours; for 'tis ill hap
If they hold when their ladies bid 'em clap.

7 that: *so that*

FINIS.

NOTES

Dramatis Personæ, omitted in the Folio, were first supplied by Rowe in 1709.

The Prologue. For general discussion of authorship, see Appendix C. It may be well, however, to state here that the question of the authorship of many parts of this play is undecided. For a hundred and fifty years Shakespeare's authorship of the *Prologue* has been denied. In the eighteenth century Dr. Samuel Johnson attributed it to Fletcher; in the nineteenth, it has been given to Ben Jonson, and to Chapman; in the twentieth, to Massinger. Besides the *Induction* to *2 Henry IV* there are only three other prologues in Shakespeare's works, those to *Troilus and Cressida, Romeo and Juliet* and *Henry V.* In each case the prologue serves to explain the play. Here it is actually misleading, since the last lines of the *Prologue* promise us a tragedy and the Fifth Act is far from tragic. And the tone of this *Prologue* is curiously apologetic.

Pro. 9. *May here find truth too.* The play of Henry VIII in 1613 had, as an alternative title, *All is True.* (See quotation from Sir Henry Wotton, Appendix B.) Some critics find here and in

'To rank our chosen truth with such a show'
(1. 18) and

'To make that only true we now intend' (1. 21)
allusions to that title. If these lines contain allusions to that title, the question of the date is settled.

Pro. 12. *shilling.* The price of admission to the best seats in the theatre. It must be remembered, however, that the purchasing power of a shilling was over eight times that at present.

Pro. 16. *In a long motley coat.* The customary costume of the stage fool.

Pro. 19. *As fool and fight is.* Dr. Johnson and later critics have regarded this gratuitous attack upon the stage fool and the stage battle as decisive evidence of the non-Shakespearean authorship of the *Prologue*, because both fools and fights are very often used by Shakespeare. It is possible that the lines, 14-16, may be an attack upon Samuel Rowley's *When you see me you know me*. (See Appendix B.)

Pro. 22. *Will leave us.* Awkward construction. The whole line, 21, is in apposition with *opinion*. The passage, 17-22, may then be paraphrased: gentle hearers, you must understand that to rank our play with a foolish comedy is, besides forfeiting our intelligence and our reputation for presenting historical truth, to lose us our friends.

Pro. 25, 26. *think ye see. see—story* are bad rimes. Theobald emends *think before ye—story;* Heath, *think ye see—history*. Actually, these rimes indicate merely that the Prologue was written hastily, not that there was an error in the printing.

I. i. S. d. *London. An Antechamber in the Palace.* The Folio, here as elsewhere, omits any indication of place. Unlike our modern stage with its elaborate sets of scenery, the Shakespearean stage was comparatively bare, with an apron projecting out into the pit. In all probability the authors had no particular place here in mind. If a particular palace must be mentioned, it was presumably that at Greenwich, to which the King, according to Holinshed, returned after the Field of the Cloth of Gold, June, 1520. It could not have been Bridewell, as has been suggested, because that palace was not built until two years later. The question is of no importance.

I. i. S. d. *Enter the Duke of Norfolk.* Thomas Howard (1443-1524), was created Duke of Norfolk in 1514 in recognition of his having won the Battle of Flodden Field. His son, the father of the poet Surrey, married Elizabeth, the eldest daughter of the Duke of Buckingham in 1513. Thus there was a close tie between the Duke of Norfolk and the Duke of Buckingham, in spite of which it was Norfolk who presided at Buckingham's trial and received as recompense part of the latter's sequestered estates. The authors seem unaware of this connection between the two noblemen: Norfolk's part in Buckingham's trial is ignored, and they seem unconscious of the difference of thirty-five years between the two speakers. Norfolk is an old man, seventy-seven, and as he died in 1524 his appearance in III. ii. is an anachronism. Historically it was Buckingham, not Norfolk, that accompanied Henry to France.

I. i. S. d. *Duke of Buckingham*. Edward Stafford (1478-1521), third Duke of Buckingham. The authors follow Holinshed in attributing Buckingham's fall to the hatred of Wolsey; there is slight foundation for this idea.

I. i. S. d. *Lord Abergavenny*. George Neville (1471-1535) was a son-in-law of the Duke of Buckingham. He was imprisoned in 1521 for complicity in Buckingham's treason, but was pardoned in March, 1522.

I. i. 6. *Those suns of glory*. Francis I, King of France, and Henry VIII, King of England.

I. i. 7. *vale of Andren*. Altered in the Second Folio to Vale of Arde, but Andren is copied from Holinshed. It is the valley separating Guynes, a town in Picardy which then belonged to the English, from Arde (or Ardres), a town also in Picardy belonging to the French. It was the locality selected for the interview between the two kings, from the seventh to the fourteenth of June, 1520, called from the magnificence of the appointments the 'Field of the Cloth of Gold.' The interview had little political significance. The time of this scene is approximately the fall of 1520.

I. i. 12. *All the whole time.* Incorrect. Buckingham was present at the Field of the Cloth of Gold; it was Norfolk that remained behind in England.

I. i. 18. *its.* Both the First and Second Folios read *it's*. The neuter possessive pronoun *its* was at this time slowly replacing the older neuter pronoun *his,* as used, for example, in l. 45 of this scene. This is the only case in Shakespeare's works where *its* is used absolutely.

I. i. 38. *Bevis.* The hero of the old tale *Bevis of Hamptoun*, a person that performs miraculous feats.

I. i. 42-47. *All was royal.* The assignment of speeches here is that of the Folio. Since Theobald, every editor has accepted his change which gives *All was royal . . . function* to Norfolk and *As you guess* to Buckingham. The Folio reading is restored on the general principle that unnecessary tampering with the text as given is unjustifiable. In addition, there is a gain in the original reading. Buckingham's emphasis on *royal* gives the actor his first opportunity to show the character's love of rank. Buckingham's speech is, then, one of acquiescence; the performance has been carried out as it should have been. On the other hand, Norfolk, who knows of Buckingham's hatred to Wolsey, to this expressed approval replies maliciously 'As you would suppose when you consider you planned it.' The Folio reading consequently makes a more dramatic scene.

I. i. 63. *Out of his self-drawing web.* The Folio here reads:

Out of his self-drawing web. O gives us note.

Capell's emendation is here followed. *A' gives us note* means that he himself tells us that, spider-like, he has created his own greatness.

King Henry the Eighth

I. i. 76-80. *for the most part such, etc.* This speech is marked by the incoherence of anger. *Such* is the object of the verb *papers; letter* is the subject of the verb *must fetch; such* is the antecedent of *him.* The meaning is: generally he lists (papers) such persons as he both wishes to tax heavily and at the same time give little honor to, and his own handwriting (letter) cheats them into incurring this expense, now that the Board of the Council is out of the way. By putting this passage into blank verse the authors cannot be said to have improved upon the clarity of Holinshed:

'The peeres of the realme receiuing letters to prepare themselues to attend the king in this iournie, and no necessarie cause expressed, why nor wherefore; seemed to grudge, that such a costlie iournie should be taken in hand to their importunate charges and expenses, without consent of the whole boord of the councell.' Holinshed (1587), p. 855.

I. i. 86. *minister communication.* These speeches of Buckingham seem to be derived from the passage from Holinshed continuing that quoted in the preceding note:

'But namelie the duke of Buckingham, being a man of a loftie courage, but not most liberall, sore repined that he should be at so great charges for his furniture foorth at this time, saieng; that he knew not for what cause so much monie should be spent about the sight of a vaine talke to be had, and communication to be ministred of things of no importance. Wherefore he sticked not to saie, that it was an intollerable matter to obeie such a vile and importunate person.'

I. i. 90. *hideous storm.* Holinshed (1587), p. 860: 'On Mondaie, the eighteenth of June, was such an hideous storme of wind and weather, that manie coniectured it did prognosticate trouble and hatred shortlie after to follow between princes.'

I. i. 95. *For France hath flaw'd the league.* Holinshed (1587), p. 872:

'Many complaints were made by the merchants to the king and his councell of the Frenchmen, which spoiled them by sea of their goods. . . . The sixt of March, the French king commanded all Englishmens goods being in Burdeaux to be attached, and put under arrest. . . . The king, understanding how his subiects were handled at Burdeaux by the French kings commandement, in breach of the league, the French ambassadour was called before the councell. . . .' As this was March, 1522, and Buckingham was executed on Friday, May 17, 1521, the authors of the play have muddled their dates.

I. i. 97. *Th' ambassador is silenc'd.* Holinshed (1587), p. 873:

'The ambassadour in words so well as he could excused his master, but in the end hee was commanded to keepe his house.'

I. i. 115. *The Duke of Buckingham's surveyor.* Holinshed (1587), p. 862:

'. . . The cardinall boiling in hatred against the duke of Buckingham, and thirsting for his bloud, deuised to make Charles Kneuet, that had beene the dukes surueior, and put from him (as ye haue heard) an instrument to bring the duke to destruction.'

Holinshed borrowed this explanation of Buckingham's fall from Polydore Vergil, a personal enemy of Wolsey. Modern investigation has shown that Wolsey's hatred was not the chief cause of the tragedy.

I. i. 120. *This butcher's cur.* Wolsey's father sold meat among other things. His will shows him to have been a successful retail grocer and butcher, and the Ipswich town records prove that he was not overscrupulous. Wolsey was often taunted with his lowly origin.

> 'How be it the primordyall
> Of his wretched originall,
> And his base progeny,
> And his gresy genealogy,
> He came of the sank royall (royal blood),
> That was cast out of a bochers stall.'
> Skelton's *Why Come Ye not to Court*.

I. i. 138. *Ipswich*. Ipswich was Wolsey's birthplace.

I. i. 172. *count-cardinal*. The title is hyphenated because a secular title is joined to an ecclesiastical one. Wolsey was both Archbishop of York and Count of Hexamshire.

I. i. 176. *Charles the emperor*. Charles V, Emperor of the Holy Roman Empire and King of Spain. His mother, Joanna, was a sister of Katharine of Aragon, wife of Henry VIII. He landed at Dover, May 26, 1520. The real and pretended motives for this visit are taken from Holinshed.

I. i. 183. *He privily*. *He* was omitted in the First Folio, but supplied in the Second.

I. i. 197 S. d. *Enter Brandon*. A Sir Thomas Brandon is mentioned by Holinshed as Master of the King's Horse. Yet, according to Holinshed, the arrest was made by Sir Henry Marny, Captain of the King's Guard. There is no dramatic reason for this change of persons; it merely shows that the dramatists worked up the material for the play rapidly.

I. i. 200. *Hereford*. The Folio misprints Hertford.

I. i. 204-206. *I am sorry, etc.* Two coördinate clauses. I am sorry to see that you are taken prisoner and to be an eye-witness to the event.

I. i. 211. *Lord Abergavenny*. The Folio spells the name Aburgany, a spelling that indicates the pronunciation. The fact of the arrest is taken from

Holinshed, 'and so likewise was lord Montacute, and both led to the Tower.'

I. i. 218. *John de la Car.* Taken from Holinshed, 'maister John de la Car alias de la Court.' John Delacourt acted as the intermediary between the Duke and Nicholas Hopkins, the Carthusian monk. Cf. n. on I. i. 221.

I. i. 219. *One Gilbert Peck, his chancellor.* Both Folios here read 'councellour.' This was corrected by Theobald from Holinshed. But there was a double error, since the name of the Duke's chancellor given by Holinshed is Gilbert Perke. Apparently 'Peck' is a misprint for Perk. Really the chancellor was Robert Gilbert. This mistake probably arose from the fact that in one of the state papers he is called 'Robert Gilbert clerk, then his chancellor.' Hall mistook 'clerk' for a name, and misprinted it Perke. Holinshed copied Hall, and the dramatists followed Holinshed. But a few paragraphs farther on, Holinshed gives both the name and title correctly: 'the said duke had sent his chancellour Robert Gilbert chapleine.' This is another indication that the dramatists had not read Holinshed carefully.

I. i. 221. *Nicholas Hopkins.* The Folios read Michaell. Theobald corrected this to Nicholas, following Holinshed. Hopkins, a monk of the Charterhouse at Henton, was a religious enthusiast, with gift of prophecy. Unintentionally he brought the Duke into danger and died broken-hearted.

I. i. 225. *instant.* These lines, 224-226, develop an elaborate meteorological figure. This very instant, eclipsing the clear sun of my prosperity, throws a cloud upon my figure and makes me only the shadow of what I was.

I. i. 226. *My lord.* The Folio, which reads *lords,* is obviously incorrect, because, as Abergavenny is

King Henry the Eighth

arrested with him and Brandon accompanies him, there is only one person, Norfolk, left on the stage.

I. ii. S. d. *The Council Chamber.* These locations of the scenes are later additions. On the Elizabethan stage there was no front curtain and ordinarily no intermission. As Buckingham and Abergavenny are led off at one side, with Norfolk following, trumpets are heard and the King enters from the other side. Sir Thomas Lovell was the Constable of the Tower. The scene follows the long account of the charges against Buckingham as given in Holinshed, with the important exception that the petition of Katharine and her attack upon Wolsey are the creation of the dramatists.

I. ii. 8 S. d. *Suffolk.* Charles Brandon, created Duke of Suffolk in 1514, married Mary Tudor, Henry's sister, the dowager Queen of France.

I. ii. 8 S. d. *King riseth from his state.* The 'state' was a raised throne with a canopy. This had been brought on by stage hands after the end of the first scene.

I. ii. 20. *there have been commissions.* This account is taken from Holinshed (1587), p. 891. But the chronology is confused. The commissions were sent in March, 1525, four years after Buckingham's death. But for this there is the dramatic reason that antedating these events enables Katharine to plead both for the people and for Buckingham, and by so doing to intensify Wolsey's dislike of her.

I. ii. 129. *Stand forth.* J. S. Brewer comments on this scene as follows:

'It will be remembered that in Shakespeare's play the Duke is declared guilty by the King at a meeting of the Privy Council, even before his regular trial had taken place;—a process altogether informal. In the Council Chamber in which Queen Katharine and Wolsey are present, the King is represented as conducting the examination of the Duke's surveyor,

Charles Knyvet, in person. The Duke has no one there to defend him; the witnesses are not subjected to cross-examination, nor is any attempt made to ascertain the accuracy of their charges, or to test their honesty and good faith by the methods now adopted in similar cases. The Duke's guilt is assumed upon their unsupported assertions. In this travesty of justice, the Queen is the only person who appears to retain any sense of what is due to reason and equity; but she is too feeble an advocate, too much bewildered by the sophistry which she feels, but is unable to unravel, to render the accused any effectual help. Besides, when kings sit in council, who shall contradict them? When their minds are already made up, "God mend all," is the natural and sole reflection which presents itself to the thoughts of inferiors. Strange as this proceeding may appear, it is not due merely to the poet's imagination. It presents us with a general likeness of State prosecutions in the Tudor times. The presumption that men are innocent until they are legally proved to be guilty, the facilities granted to the accused for substantiating his innocence by retaining the ablest advocate, the methods for sifting evidence now in use, had no existence then. In crimes against the sovereign, real or supposed, men were presumed to be guilty until they proved themselves to be innocent, and that proof was involved in endless difficulties. What advocate or what witness would have ventured to brave the displeasure of a Tudor king, by appearing in defense of a criminal, on whose guilt the King had pronounced already? With the exception of making Wolsey present at the examination of the Duke's servants and surveyor, Shakespeare has strictly adhered to facts in this preliminary examination of the Duke's servants.'

(J. S. Brewer, *The Reign of Henry VIII,* I. 383.)

I. ii. 147. *Henton.* This, the Folio reading, was

King Henry the Eighth

altered by Theobald to 'Hopkins.' But as he was often called Henton from the monastery to which he belonged, 'there is no need to amend the text.' (Gollancz.) Cf. I. i. 221 and note.

I. ii. 151-171. These twenty lines are merely Holinshed (1587), p. 864, in blank verse.

I. ii. 164. *confession's seal.* Theobald's emendation of the Folio's reading *Commissions seal.* It comes from Holinshed, 'under the seal of confession.'

I. ii. 170. *To gain.* The word *gain* was added in the Fourth Folio to complete the meter.

I. ii. 172. *You were the duke's surveyor.* The accusation against Knyvet is taken from Holinshed.

I. ii. 177-186. This speech is versified Holinshed.

I. ii. 179. *for him.* Capell's emendation for the *for this* of the Folio.

I. ii. 190. *Bulmer.* The Folio printer transposed the letters, so that the name reads *Blumer.*

I. ii. 213. *by day and night.* An exclamation. Cf. *Hamlet,* I. v. 164, 'O day and night, but this is wondrous strange!'

I. iii. The third scene, which serves only as a prelude to the fourth, is typical of Fletcher's style. It has been explained by some commentators as being an attack upon the courtiers of James I. Although there is no dramatic reason for its existence, it is an expansion of one paragraph of Holinshed (1587), p. 850, and of another on p. 852. Owing to the fact that the dramatists skipped back and forth in versifying the passages from Holinshed, the chronology is hopeless. This scene was in 1519. At this time the Lord Chamberlain was Charles Somerset, Earl of Worcester, and Sir William Sands (or Sandys) had not been raised to the nobility.

I. iii. 12, 13. *spavin Or springhalt.* Verplanck's emendation for the Folio,

... the Spauen
A Spring-halt ...

because the two diseases are different, although each causes lameness in a horse.

I. iii. 25. *Of fool and feather.* Alluding to the long feathers worn in the hats.

I. iii. 27. *as fights and fireworks.* There had been jousting at the Field of the Cloth of Gold, and the interview had ended with a display of fireworks.

I. iii. 30. *tall stockings.* The extreme of the fashion was very short puffed trousers and long stockings, reaching above the knee.

I. iii. 63. *My barge stays.* Before the Victoria Embankment was built, the palaces along the river front had steps leading down to the river, because the ordinary means of travel was by boat.

I. iv. This scene, also by Fletcher, is a dramatization of the passage from Holinshed (1587), pp. 921 ff. But Holinshed's *Chronicle* is itself a compilation from a number of previous works. This particular passage is an almost verbatim reprint from George Cavendish's *Life of Cardinal Wolsey.* According to Hall, the entertainment took place January 3, 1527. Consequently chronological order in the play is incorrect in placing it before Buckingham's death. This error arose from the fact that Holinshed, after he had finished a year-by-year account of Wolsey's career, summarized his character, drawing from Cavendish. Consequently in this part of Holinshed no dates are given to the events described. This error in dating causes another, namely, that in 1527 the Lord Chamberlain and Lord Sandys were not different persons, as Sandys had become Lord Chamberlain the year before. Sir Henry Guilford was Master of Horse.

York Place, then the residence of Wolsey, later became Whitehall, the royal palace. Cf. IV. i. 95-97.

I. iv. 49 S. d. *Chambers discharged.* This appears to have been the occasion of the conflagration which destroyed the Globe Theatre. See Appendix B, p. 150.

I. iv. 75. *The fairest hand.* Anne Boleyn's presence at this entertainment is an invention of the dramatists. There is no indication in Holinshed that she was there.

I. iv. 96. *And not to kiss you.* Kissing before the dance was the custom. If he had not kissed her, he would have been 'unmannerly.'

II. i. This scene (by Fletcher), while scarcely advancing the action of the drama, is yet finely effective, taken by itself. It is a close dramatization from Holinshed (1587), p. 865, even to the extent of keeping many of the original phrases.

II. i. 18. *To have brought.* The first three Folios read *To him brought;* the correction was made in the Fourth.

II. i. 43, 44. *Earl Surrey was sent thither, and in haste too, Lest he should help his father.* Thomas Howard, Earl of Surrey and in 1524 Duke of Norfolk, had married Elizabeth Stafford, the eldest daughter of the Duke of Buckingham.

II. i. 53. *The mirror of all courtesy.* 'He is tearmed in the books of the law in the said thirteenth yeare of Henrie the eight (where his arreignement is liberallie set downe) to be the floure and mirror of all courtesie.' Holinshed (1587), p. 870.

II. i. 53 S. d. *the axe with the edge towards him.* This indicated that the prisoner had been condemned.

II. i. 53 S. d. *Sir William Sandys.* The same character that has figured in Act I as Lord Sandys, only here his title is correctly given. Theobald corrected the Folio, which reads *Walter*.

II. i. 67. *evils.* Some commentators have wished to take *evils* in this passage and in *Measure for Measure,* II. ii. 172, in the Elizabethan sense of *privy* or *out-house*. This meaning at best is doubtful. Here, however, where the style is both elliptical and metaphorical, the usual sense of *crimes* seems the simpler reading.

II. i. 103. *Edward Bohun*. Buckingham's surname was Stafford, although he was a remote descendant of the Bohun family. The mistake, however, is in Holinshed.

II. i. 107. *My noble father*. Henry Stafford, High Constable of England and Duke of Buckingham, raised a revolt against Richard III, was betrayed by his servant, Humphrey Banaster, and beheaded in 1483, 'without arreignement or iudgement.'

II. i. 148-153. This passage is versified Holinshed (1587), p. 897.

II. i. 160. *Cardinal Campeius*. Cardinal Lorenzo Campeggio was sent by the Pope, Clement VII, to judge the question jointly with Wolsey. As the Pope had withheld the power to make a decision, the trial was necessarily adjourned.

II. i. 164. *The archbishopric of Toledo*. This motivation of Wolsey's conduct is taken from Holinshed.

II. ii. 18, 19. *No; his conscience Has crept too near another lady*. As has been pointed out by Mr. Vaughan, this speech of Suffolk is an aside, and Norfolk's ' 'Tis so' is in agreement with the opinion of the Chamberlain. This speech is incongruous coming from the mouth of the historical Duke of Suffolk!

II. ii. 21. *That blind priest*. Reckless, because he cannot see. But the adjective suggests the familiar figure of Fortune, with her wheel.

II. ii. 62 S. d. At the back of the Elizabethan stage there was a gallery. Under the gallery was a recess, screened by curtains. This recess here is used as the King's study. And it is upon the gallery that the King and Butts play in Act V. ii.

King Henry the Eighth

II. ii. 85. *have-at-him.* A thrust. This is Dyce's emendation of the Folio 'If it doe; Ile venture one; haue at him.'

II. ii. 109. *Gardiner.* Stephen Gardiner (1483-1555), Trinity College, Cambridge, early distinguished himself as a student in Civil and Canon Law. As such, he was employed by Henry as an agent in the divorce proceedings. After Wolsey's death he was rewarded by being made Bishop of Winchester (1531). He later became an opponent of Cranmer and the Reformation, was imprisoned throughout the reign of Edward VI, and was one of the chief counsellors of Mary. Since it was in her reign that the Protestants were persecuted, Gardiner was popularly held responsible and generally hated.

II. ii. 112. Taken from Holinshed.

II. ii. 122. *Doctor Pace.* Richard Pace (1482?-1536), a celebrated scholar and writer, succeeded the famous John Colet as Dean of St. Paul's. He was also Dean of Exeter and of Salisbury. He had been sent on many embassies, but in 1525 he was forced to return to England owing to mental derangement. Holinshed is reporting popular gossip in crediting this insanity to the persecutions of the Cardinal, but an examination of the state papers does not justify such a conclusion.

II. ii. 139. *Blackfriars.* Before the Reformation the monastic establishment of the Dominicans, between Ludgate Hill and the Thames. The locality is still marked by Blackfriars Bridge.

II. iii. This scene, which has no structural importance in the play, is used to characterize Anne Boleyn. Except for the brief conversation in I. iv. and her appearance in the procession in IV. i., this is her only scene. The contrast between the dramatic importance given to Katharine by the dramatist and that given to Anne, the mother of Queen Elizabeth, is curious.

II. iii. 1-11. The ejaculatory form of Anne's speech expresses her emotion, and also marks the reappearance of Shakespeare's style.

II. iii. 36. *three-pence.* This is an anachronism, because 'the first large and regular coinage of threepences took place in the reign of Elizabeth' (Fairholt).

II. iii. 44. *Ever to get a boy.* An allusion to Henry's desire for a male heir.

II. iii. 46. *little England.* Steevens suggested that 'little England' may be Pembrokeshire. This interpretation is over-subtle as the Old Lady is not supposed to know that Anne was about to be created Marchioness of Pembroke and certainly the audience does not know it.

II. iii. 47. *emballing.* Explained by commentators as a reference to the ball, the symbol of power, placed in the hand of the sovereign at the coronation. It was not used at the coronation of a queen-consort; Anne was given a dove upon an ivory staff. Merely an indelicate joke.

II. iii. 48. *Carnarvonshire.* A barren county in Wales, in contrast to fertile England.

II. iii. 61. *of you.* The Folio reads

'Commends his good opinion of you, to you;'

Presumably the 'to you' is an error of the typesetter, although the verse of this play is so ragged that the dramatists may have written it so.

II. iii. 63. *Marchioness of Pembroke.* Taken from Holinshed.

II. iii. 78. *a gem.* An allusion to Queen Elizabeth.

II. iii. 86. *fie, fie.* The Folio gives three *fie's;* but the third is an extra syllable in the line.

II. iii. 92. *mud in Egypt.* The wealth of Egypt is due to the mud deposited by the overflowing Nile.

II. iv. S. d. The location of this scene is taken from Holinshed. Bishop of Canterbury is an obvious error for Archbishop of Canterbury. At this time, June 21, 1529, the Archbishop of Canterbury was William Warham; the Bishop of Lincoln, John Longland; the Bishop of Ely, Nicholas West; the Bishop of Rochester, John Fisher; and the Bishop of Saint Asaph was Henry Standish. The details of this procession are taken from Holinshed. In an uneducated age, the meaning of events was explained to the crowd by symbols. The *purse* was carried to represent the Treasury; the *great seal* signified that Wolsey was Lord Chancellor; the *hat,* that he was a cardinal; the *two crosses* represented his archbishopric and his commission from the Pope as legate; the *silver mace* was the emblem of authority; the *two pillars,* the insignia of a cardinal. The procession, then, was a visible representation of Wolsey's position in the Church and in the State. The scene is a dramatization of Holinshed (1587), pp. 907, 908; the speeches are little more than a versifying of Holinshed's prose.

II. iv. 11. *Sir, I desire.* Compare this speech with Holinshed: 'Sir (quoth she) I desire you to doo me justice and right, and take some pitie upon me, for I am a poore woman, and a stranger, borne out of your dominion, having here no indifferent counsell, and assurance of freendship. Alas sir, what have I offended you, or what occasion of displeasure have I shewed you, intending thus to put me from you after this sort? I take God to my judge, I have beene to you a true and humble wife, ever conformable to your will and pleasure, that never contraried or gainesaid any thing thereof, and being alwaies contented with all things wherein you had any delight, whether little or much, without grudge or displeasure, I loved for your sake all them whom you loved, whether they were my freends or enimies,' etc., etc. The other speeches are equally close.

II. iv. 35. *many children.* Of the five children

that Katharine had borne, only one survived, Mary. She succeeded her half-brother, Edward VI, on the throne.

II. iv. 111-113. *your words, Domestics to you, etc.* Your words, like household servants, perform any service that your will desires.

II. iv. 125. *Gent. Ush.* From Holinshed, the name of the gentleman usher is Griffith. He appears again in IV. ii.

II. iv. 170. *Bishop of Bayonne.* As a matter of fact, Cavendish, who is Holinshed's authority here, was mistaken; it was not Du Bellay, Bishop of Bayonne, but Grammont, Bishop of Tarbes, that came on this embassy.

II. iv. 180. *bosom of my conscience.* Holinshed's phrase is 'bottom of my conscience.'

II. iv. 223. *drives.* The old Northern English plural, common in Shakespeare. Compare 'compels' in I. ii. 57.

II. iv. 236. *Cranmer.* Cranmer was then abroad, collecting opinions concerning the validity of the King's marriage.

III. i. The location of this scene is taken from Holinshed, and is dramatized from the account there given.

III. i. 23. *But all hoods make not monks.* The Latin form of this proverb, *cucullus non facit monachum,* is quoted also in *Measure for Measure* and in *Twelfth Night.*

III. i. 40. *Tanta est erga te, etc.* 'So great is the honesty of our purpose toward you, most noble Queen.' As Holinshed says only that they started to speak Latin, these words are the creation of the dramatists.

III. i. 60. *your cause.* The Second Folio corrects the First, which reads *our cause.*

III. i. 144. *Ye have angels' faces.* Katharine is a

Spaniard. She is here alluding to Pope Gregory's famous exclamation, *Non Angli sed angeli.*

III. ii. This scene, with the possible exception of the death of Katharine, IV. ii, is the most famous one in the play. Nichol Smith divides it into: (1) the interview between the King and Wolsey; (2) the interview between the nobles and Wolsey; (3) the interview between Wolsey and Cromwell. Of these three only the second is taken directly from Holinshed, but details in the first and third are from Holinshed's summary of Wolsey's character.

The chronology is hopelessly confused. 'Lord' Surrey, the Earl of Surrey, was after 1524 the poet Surrey, because his grandfather, the Norfolk of the First Act, had died in that year and transmitted the ducal title to the poet's father, the Norfolk of this scene. More's appointment as Chancellor followed Wolsey's death, and Cranmer was consecrated Archbishop of Canterbury, March 30, 1533. For dramatic effect events thus separated by years are condensed into one scene.

III. ii. 23. *Not to come off.* In the speech, the pronouns are ambiguous. No, he (Wolsey) is settled in his (the King's) displeasure, not to escape.

III. ii. 30. *The cardinal's letters.* Holinshed (1587), p. 909: 'he required the pope by letters and secret messengers, that in anie wise he should defer the iudgement of the diuorce, till he might frame the kings mind to his purpose.'

III. ii. 42. *Would he had!* As Anne Boleyn was the niece of the 'Lord Surrey' of the play, the exclamation is natural enough. The dramatists, however, show no knowledge of this relationship. Apparently the only value of the information is its relation to the fall of Wolsey.

III. ii. 51. *Will fall some blessing.* An obvious allusion to Queen Elizabeth.

III. ii. 56. *Cardinal Campeius.* The dramatists here abandon Holinshed, who expressly states that Campeggio took a formal leave of the King. Boswell-Stone suggests that this idea comes from Foxe, according to whose account Campeggio 'craftily shifted hym self out of the realme before the day came appointed for determination, leauing his suttle felow behynd hym to wey with the king in the meane time.'

III. ii. 69-71. *Katharine no more Shall be call'd queen, etc.* Holinshed (1587), p. 929: 'It was also enacted the same time that queene Katharine should no more be called queene, but princesse Dowager, as the widow of prince Arthur.'

III. ii. 86. *Duchess of Alençon.* This is an anachronism, since Margaret, Duchess of Alençon, was married to Henry d'Albret, King of Navarre, January, 1527.

III. ii. 100. *A spleeny Lutheran.* According to Foxe, and the Elizabethan tradition, Anne Boleyn was an enthusiastic champion of the Protestant Reformation.

III. ii. 107 S. d. *Enter King, reading of a schedule.* This incident never happened to Wolsey, but, as Steevens first pointed out, Holinshed chronicles one like it that did happen to the Bishop of Durham in 1523. After Wolsey's fall, however, an elaborate inventory of the contents of Hampton Court was made by the King's order.

III. ii. 167-172. *My sovereign, etc.* The English here is careless, but the meaning is obvious. My sovereign, I confess that your royal favors, which were showered upon me daily, have been more than my earnest efforts could requite; your favors went beyond any man's endeavors; my endeavors have always come short of my desires, but they have kept pace with my ability.

III. ii. 189-191. Should, not from duty, but from a supreme love, belong to me above all men.

III. ii. 193. *that am, have, and will be.* This, the reading of the Folio, has been the cause of more emendation than any line of the play. Yet in all probability the line is as the authors wrote it. The expression is elliptical with the forms of the verb 'labour' omitted. The passage in full means: 'I do profess, that for your highness' good I ever laboured more than for my own good: that I am labouring, have laboured, and will be labouring.'

III. ii. 232. *Asher-house.* A curious error, because Asher (or Esher) House was the official residence of the Bishop of Winchester and at this time the Bishop of Winchester was Wolsey himself. Of course, the authors meant by 'Bishop of Winchester' Stephen Gardiner, but he did not become Bishop until 1531, after Wolsey's death. Wolsey did go to Asher, according to Holinshed.

III. ii. 296. *Worse than the sacring bell.* In the Roman Catholic service, the sacring bell is rung at the elevation of the Host during the Mass, or before the Sacraments when they are carried through the streets. There is no historical truth to this particular accusation, although Wolsey's life was not chaste.

III. ii. 311. *First, that, etc.* This list of accusations is taken from Holinshed.

III. ii. 344. *Chattels.* Theobald's emendation for the Folio reading, *Castles,* taken from Holinshed's enumeration: 'to forfeit all his lands, tenements, goods, and cattels.'

III. ii. 372. *he falls like Lucifer.* Isaiah 14. 12: 'How art thou fallen from heaven, O Lucifer, son of the morning!'

III. ii. 450. *Thou fall'st a blessed martyr.* This line is prophecy, after the event. Cromwell, who from his suppression of the monasteries was considered to be a supporter of the Reformation, was executed in 1540.

III. ii. 456-458. *Had I but serv'd my God, etc.* This, the most quoted passage in the play, is adapted from Holinshed (1587, p. 917): 'Master Kinston (quoth the cardinall) I see the matter how it is framed: but if I had serued God as diligentlie as I have doone the king, he would not haue given me ouer in my greie haires.'

IV. i. S. d. The locality of this scene is inferred from the scene itself. The coronation took place June 1, 1533.

IV. i. 4. *At our last encounter.* The two gentlemen last appeared in II. i., when Buckingham came forth after his trial. Historically twelve years separated these two events.

IV. i. 15. *Of those that claim.* By long custom the right to perform the various services is vested in certain families. Holinshed (1587), p. 930:

'In the beginning of Maie, the king caused open proclamations to be made, that all men that claimed to doo anie seruice, or execute anie office at the solemne feast of the coronation by the waie of tenure, grant, or prescription, should put their grant three weeks after Easter in the Starre-chamber before Charles duke of Suffolke, for that time high steward of England, and the lord chancellor and other commissioners. The duke of Norfolke claimed to be erle mershall, and to exercise his office at that feast; the erle of Arundell claimed to be high butler, and to exercise the same; the erle of Oxford claimed to be chamberlaine; the viscount Lisle claimed to be pantler; the lord Aburgauennie to be chief larderer; and the lord Braie claimed to be almoner, and sir Henrie Wiat knight claimed to be ewrer. All these noble personages desired their offices with their fees.

'Beside these, the maior of London claimed to serue the queene with a cup of gold, and a cup of assaie of the same, and that twelve citizens should attend on the cupboord, and the maior to have the cup and cup of assaie for his labor: which petition was allowed. The five ports claimed to beare a canopie ouer the queens head the daie of the coronation with foure guilt belles, and to haue the same for a reward, which to them was allowed. Diuerse other put in petie claimes which were not allowed, bicause they seemed onlie to be doone at the kings coronation.'

IV. i. 27. *Dunstable.* The court was held at Dunstable Priory, in Bedfordshire, six miles from Ampthill Castle, a royal residence.

IV. i. 34. *Kimbolton.* In the fall of 1535 Katharine at her own request had been removed to Kimbolton Castle in Huntingdonshire, then belonging to the Wingfield family. The Folio spells the word 'Kymmalton.'

IV. i. 36 S. d. *The Order of the Coronation.* The details of this procession, which is the reason for the scene, are taken from Holinshed. But they are somewhat changed to suit the stage. Thus the Earl of Surrey carries the rod with the dove, instead of the Earl of Arundell, and the Duke of Norfolk the staff of marshalship, instead of Sir William Howard, probably, as Wright suggests, to avoid introducing two new characters. Possibly to avoid confusion in the personages, the Earl of Oxford, then High Chamberlain, who carries the crown on a cushion, is also omitted.

The 'Collars of Esses' were so called because the links in the chains were in the shape of the letter S.

The 'Cinque-ports,' Dover, Hastings, Romney, Hythe and Sandwich, have the privilege of sending representatives to carry the canopy at the coronation. Cf. note on IV. i. 15.

IV. i. 62 ff. The 'third Gentleman' is obviously introduced to give an account of the coronation to the audience. The details of the scene follow Holinshed, as usual.

IV. i. 94. *York-place, where the feast is held.* After Wolsey's fall, York-place, the official residence of Wolsey as Archbishop of York, was annexed to the property of the Crown, and became the royal palace of Whitehall. It served as a royal residence until it burned in 1697. Only the banqueting hall still remains, now on Horseguards Ave. The coronation feast, however, was not held in Whitehall; as Holinshed correctly states, it was held in Westminster Hall. The confusion in the play may have arisen from the fact that in Holinshed there is also a long detailed account of the procession escorting the Queen from the Tower to Westminster. At the end of that, the first procession, he states that Anne 'withdrew herself with a few ladies to the Whitehall and so to her chamber.'

IV. i. 101. *Stokesly and Gardiner.* John Stokesly was made Bishop of London in 1530; Stephen Gardiner, Bishop of Winchester in 1531. As Gardiner was considered an enemy of the Reformation, he was 'no great good lover' of Cranmer. Thus l. 104 prepares for the first scene in Act V.

IV. i. 108. *Thomas Cromwell.* Cromwell was made a member of the Privy Council in 1531 and Master of the Jewel House in 1532.

IV. ii. 6, 7. *Cardinal Wolsey, Was dead.* For dramatic reasons the death of Wolsey precedes that of Katharine by only a short interval. Historically, Wolsey died November 29, 1530, whereas this scene would have occurred in January, 1536.

IV. ii. 9. *tell me how he died.* This account is condensed from Holinshed (1587), p. 917.

IV. ii. 31. *So may he rest, etc.* Katharine's characterization of Wolsey is, point by point, taken from Holinshed (1587), p. 922. 'This cardinall (as you may perceive in this storie) was of a great stomach, for he compted himselfe equall with princes, & by

King Henry the Eighth 143

craftie suggestion gat into his hands innumerable treasure: he forced little on simonie, and was not pittifull, and stood affectionate in his owne opinion: in open presence he would lie and saie untruth, and was double both in speach and meaning: he would promise much and performe little: he was vicious of his bodie, & gaue the clergie euill example. . . .'

IV. ii. 48 ff. Griffith's commendation of Wolsey is equally taken from Holinshed (1587), p. 917: 'This cardinall (as Edward Campian in his historie of Ireland describeth him) was a man undoubtedly borne to honor: I thinke (saith he) some princes bastard, no butchers sonne, exceeding wise, faire spoken, high minded, full of reuenge, vitious of his bodie, loftie to his enemies, were they neuer so big, to those that accepted and sought his freendship woonderfull courteous, a ripe schooleman, thrall to affections, brought a bed with flatterie, insatiable to get, and more princelie in bestowing, as appeareth by his two colleges at Ipswich and Oxenford, the one ouerthrowne with his fall, the other unfinished, and yet as it lieth as an house for students, considering all the appurtenances incomparable thorough Christendome, whereof Henrie the eight is now called founder, bicause he let it stand . . . neuer happie till this his ouerthrow. Wherein he shewed such moderation, and ended so perfectlie, that the houre of his death did him more honor, than all the pompe of his life passed.'

IV. ii. 50. *From his cradle.* Many editors prefer Theobald's punctuation, which puts a period after 'cradle' instead of after 'honour.'

IV. ii. 59. *Ipswich, and Oxford.* The college founded by Wolsey at Ipswich remains only in a gatehouse; Christ Church at Oxford was founded by Wolsey and originally called Cardinal College.

IV. ii. 111. *Capucius.* Holinshed (1587), p.

939: 'The princesse Dowager lieng at Kimbolton, fell into hir last sicknesse, whereof the king being aduertised, appointed the emperors ambassador that was legier here with him named Caputius, to go to visit hir, and to do his commendations to hir, and will hir to be of good comfort.'

V. The first four scenes of this act dramatize an anecdote told by Foxe in his *Acts and Monuments of Martyrs* (usually called briefly the *Book of Martyrs*) (1583), pp. 1866 and 1867. The fifth scene is taken from Holinshed (1587), pp. 934-935.

There is no attempt at chronology. Sir Thomas Lovell died in 1524; Elizabeth was born 1533; Cromwell was executed in 1540; and the scene with Cranmer must have been in 1544 or 1545.

V. ii. 18 S. d. *Enter the King and Butts at a window above.* In the Folio there is no division between this scene and the one following. This was unfortunately introduced by White to conform to our modern stage conventions. The King and Butts appeared upon the gallery across the back of the Elizabethan stage. Then, with them in full view of the audience but out of the sight of the actors upon the stage, the council assembled below.

V. iii. 29-31. Doubtless an allusion to the Anabaptist rising in Münster under John of Leyden, 1534-1535.

V. iii. 85. *This is too much.* The Folio gives all the speeches in this scene, here assigned to the Lord Chancellor, to the Lord Chamberlain. As was pointed out by Capell, they belong rather to the Lord Chancellor because he was the presiding officer. The error was probably due to a misreading of the abbreviation Chan. into Cham. Some modern editors, however, assign one of the seven speeches to the Lord Chamberlain, since otherwise he would be silent.

King Henry the Eighth

V. iii. 133. *his place.* This is the reading of the Folio. Paraphrased, it means: now let the proudest deny that thou art his equal, that his position becomes thee. Some modern editors, however, follow Rowe's emendation, 'this place.'

V. iv. 2. *Parish-garden.* The corrupt pronunciation for Paris-garden, a place of unruly entertainment near the site of the Globe Theatre.

V. iv. 16. *May-day morning.* On the first of May it was customary to go out early into the fields to gather flowers and dew, which was considered good for the complexion.

V. iv. 23. *I am not Samson, etc.* The allusion to the proverbial strength of Samson as told in the Old Testament story is obvious. Sir Guy of Warwick is the hero of the medieval romance of the same name; one of his adventures is the killing of the giant Colbrand.

V. iv. 28. *for a cow.* A proverbial expression, still in use, it is said.

V. iv. 34. *Moorfields.* The exercising ground of the London militia.

V. iv. 35. *strange Indian.* It was the Jacobean custom to exhibit Indians, much as we do Hottentots. If the date of exhibition of such an Indian could be ascertained, it would be a clue to the troubled question of the date of the play. Compare *The Tempest*, II. ii. 29-35.

V. iv. 41. *The spoons will be the bigger.* Spoons were favorite gifts at christenings. See V. iii. 166, 167.

V. iv. 54. *Clubs.* 'Clubs' was the rallying cry of the London apprentices.

V. iv. 67, 68. *Tribulation of Tower-hill, or the Limbs of Limehouse.* These are fanciful names, alluding to unruly districts of London.

V. iv. 71. *running banquet.* The two beadles

(officers of the law) will chase them, whipping them, after the prison term of three days has expired.

V. v. Elizabeth was christened September 10, 1533.

Appendix A

Sources of the Play

The sources of *Henry VIII* are Holinshed's *Chronicle* for the first four acts and the last scene of the fifth act, and Foxe's *Book of Martyrs* for the first four scenes of the fifth act. Mr. Chambers[1] posits an earlier version of the play called by the name of Buckingham. This does not seem probable because Holinshed is not the 'source' in the rather vague sense applicable to the other plays. Here much of the play is merely Holinshed's scenes dramatized and his words put into blank verse. A fair illustration is the speech of the First Gentleman, II. ii. 149-153.

> Yes, but it held not;
> For when the king once heard it, out of anger
> He sent command to the lord mayor straight
> To stop the rumour, and allay those tongues
> That durst disperse it.

Compare this passage with Holinshed:

'The king was offended with those tales, and sent for Sir Thomas Seimor maior of the citie of London, secretlie charging him to see that the people ceased from such talke.'

But as the play covers a period of twenty-four years, over a hundred folio pages in Holinshed, the playwrights selected passages to dramatize. From this condition three criticisms follow:

(1) The chronology is hopelessly confused, as the action is compressed into six or seven days. This confusion is partly unavoidable; the changes which occur during a quarter of a century must be ignored. The characters of the first act would have actually

[1] E. K. Chambers, *The Elizabethan Stage*, Vol. 2, p. 202.

been old men or have died at the time the last must be dated. But also the playwrights did not care about the actual sequence of events, and the historical order of events is unnecessarily disarranged in the play.

(2) The characters neither develop, nor are they consistent. An illustration of the first point may be found in the treatment of the character of Henry himself. In 1520, the date of the opening of the play, he was twenty-nine years old, in the full vigor of his young manhood, athletic, fond of pleasure, and still tricked by the external; in 1544, the latest date in the play, he was old, sick, with an indomitable will and a shrewd sense that made him the most powerful personality in Europe. But the King Henry of the play is the same from the first act to the fifth. This may be due to the fact that the writers are frankly disregarding the lapse of time. The explanation for the inconsistency of the characters is quite different. The best illustration of this is to be found in the character of Wolsey. The fallen Wolsey of Act III has little in common with the arrogant prelate that plotted the fall of Buckingham. In Act III he is a heroic character with whose misfortunes the audience sympathizes; in Act I he is a tyrant, and there is no attempt to bridge this gap. These opposing interpretations of the same person are to be found in the original authority. Holinshed's work is not a history in the modern sense. A modern historian studies the period, determines the relative values of the various incidents, and presents us with a unified interpretation of the events. But this is not the method of the old chroniclers. Holinshed copies previous writers, stating the fact in the margin, but he makes no attempt to reconcile them. For the character of Wolsey he relies first upon the narrative of Polydore Vergil. The latter was an Italian who came to England about 1501. He got into trouble with

Wolsey and was put into prison by the latter. Consequently when he wrote his history of England, he gave an unfavorable account of Wolsey and imputed base motives for his actions. This account Holinshed followed. But toward the end of his account he ran into the life of Wolsey written by George Cavendish, who had been Wolsey's gentleman usher. Naturally to Cavendish Wolsey was ideal magnificence personified. Consequently when Holinshed grafted Cavendish's opinion of Wolsey's character upon the narrative of Polydore Vergil it formed an unexpected conclusion. In one scene of the play the two points of view are brought into sharp contrast. In Act IV, scene ii, Katharine is giving vent to ideas of Polydore Vergil, whereas Griffith replies by talking Cavendish.

(3) In any drama the scenes should have an organic relation, the succeeding scene should develop from those preceding, until in the last act the audience perceives the drama as a unified whole. That is far from the case here. The leading personage of the first part is Buckingham; then Wolsey takes the stage, then Katharine, and we end with Cranmer and the christening of Elizabeth. Thus the drama is not a drama at all; it is a series of almost unrelated scenes, describing events that occurred in the reign of Henry VIII, and with him as vaguely felt center. This again is due to the writers' dependence upon Holinshed. He had no philosophical conception of the reign, and they did little more than dramatize selected scenes as they came to them. According to the statements in the Prologue they regarded this dependence as a virtue. That is the obvious meaning of the line

'To make that only true we now intend,'

and the emphasis upon truth in line 9. In other words, they felt that they were following Holinshed as carefully as possible.

Appendix B

The History of the Play

On June 29, 1613, the Globe Theatre, the theatre with which Shakespeare was connected, burned to the ground, 'the house being filled with people to behold the play, viz. of Henry the Eighth.' Such is Stowe's brief account. The day following Thomas Lorkin wrote to Sir Thomas Puckering:

'No longer since than yesterday, while Burbage's company were acting at the Globe the play of Henry VIII, and there shooting off certain chambers [cannon] in way of triumph, the fire catched and fastened upon the thatch of the house, and there burned so furiously, as it consumed the whole house, all in less than two hours, the people having enough to do to save themselves.'

The most famous account is that written on July 2 by Sir Henry Wotton to his nephew:

'Now, to let matters of state sleep, I will entertain you at the present with what has happened this week at the Bankside. The King's players had a new play, called *All is True*, representing some principal pieces of the reign of Henry VIII, which was set forth with many extraordinary circumstances of pomp and majesty, even to the matting of the stage; the Knights of the Order with their Georges and garters, the Guards with their embroidered coats, and the like: sufficient in truth within a while to make greatness very familiar, if not ridiculous. Now, King Henry making a masque at the Cardinal Wolsey's house, and certain chambers being shot off at his entry, some of the paper, or other stuff, wherewith one of them was stopped, did light on the thatch, where being thought at first but an idle smoke, and their eyes more attentive to the show, it kindled inwardly, and ran round like a train, consuming within less than an hour the whole house to the very grounds. This was the fatal period of that virtuous fabric, wherein yet nothing did perish but wood and straw, and a few forsaken cloaks; only one man had his breeches set on fire, that would perhaps have broiled him, if he had not by the benefit of a provident wit put it out with bottle ale.'

There are other contemporary allusions to the famous fire, but the foregoing are the most precise. Thus there is no question that the Globe was set on fire during the performance of a play dealing with the reign of Henry VIII. Although there were other plays centering around Henry VIII at this time, the probability is that the particular play is, certainly for the most part, the one we have. Contemporary verses mention both Heminges and Condell as being the actors in it; and Heminges and Condell ten years later printed our play as belonging to the Shakespearean repertoire. In 1623 they could scarcely have forgotten the play that had proved so disastrous to them. If this is the play, either Sir Henry Wotton was mistaken about the title, or it was advertised under an alternative title *All is True,* and the lines of the Prologue may allude to this alternative title. There are two slight corroborative details. In Act I, scene iv (l. 49), a stage direction reads 'chambers discharged'; the Globe would seem, then, to have burned at the end of the first act. And the 'business' of the part of King Henry was said after the Restoration to have been handed down from Shakespeare himself.

The suggestion of Chambers and others that it was an old play revamped does not seem probable. Sir Henry Wotton speaks of it as a 'new play.' This seems borne out by internal evidence. The play apparently was thrown together hurriedly, without much planning, to meet some emergency. What that emergency was it is impossible to tell at this late date. It has been suggested that the play was written to celebrate the marriage of the Princess Elizabeth with the Elector Palatine, which took place on the fourteenth of February, 1613. But as runs were very brief in that age, it is questionable whether Wotton would have described it four months later as 'new' if that had been the case. There is no need for positing a great ceremonial, or an affair of state, to call for the play. The emergency may equally well have been purely theatrical: that the manager was disappointed in a play for which he had contracted, or that the play he had intended to produce was unavailable for one of a hundred reasons, and a new play had to be substituted. At least, *Henry VIII* shows signs of hurried work. As we do not have the manuscript, it is always possible that the obvious errors in the text are due to the mistakes of the typesetter. That is not true in some cases here. The authors themselves must be held responsible for imprisoning Wolsey in Asher House, the residence of the Bishop of Winchester, when Wolsey was himself Bishop of Winchester. Such a slip can mean only that the authors had read their Holinshed rapidly. The banquet after the coronation is plainly stated to have been held in Westminster Hall; on a preceding page, following the account of a previous procession, Holinshed tells us that Anne retired to Whitehall. Presumably the authors lost the place in the chronicle and they have put the coronation banquet in Whitehall. Sandys, who was 'Lord' Sandys in Act I, is degraded to mere knighthood in Act II. Such mistakes as these are not due to an ignorant typesetter; they are due to a writer that cares vastly more for the theatrical significance of the scene than for historical accuracy. Other errors, while possibly typographical, are probably due to careless composition. Reading the black letter of

King Henry the Eighth

Holinshed hastily, the authors transformed his phrase 'bottom of my conscience' into 'bosom of my conscience' (II. iv. 180) and his noun chattels, which he spells 'cattels,' into 'castles' (III. ii. 344). Slips like these all favor the assumption that for some reason a new play was required and authors set to work at full speed to produce one. It was written to be played, not to be read, and such errors as the foregoing, are, from the point of view of the audience, immaterial. The wonder is, not that the play is so poor, but that it is so good. The authors have succeeded in constructing a drama with pageant-like scenes and a few opportunities for good actors. These were the characteristics of it from the very beginning. According to contemporary accounts Burbage himself played in it, and Wotton stresses the elaborateness of the costumes. And these are the characteristics that have caused it to be revived over and over again. Pepys saw the great production in 1664, when Betterton played the King; Harris, Wolsey; Smith, Buckingham; and Mrs. Betterton, Queen Katharine. His comment is unfavorable:

'But my wife and I rose from table, pretending business, and went to the Duke's house (Lincoln's Inn Fields), the first play I have been at these six months, according to my last vowe, and here saw the so much cried-up play of "Henry the Eighth"; which, though I went with resolution to like it, is so simple a thing made up of a great many patches, that, besides the shows and procession in it, there is nothing in the world good or well done. Thence mightily dissatisfied back at night to my uncle Wight's. . . .'

Four years later, however, he is not so fastidious:

'After dinner, my wife and I to the Duke's playhouse, and there did see "King Harry the Eighth"; and was mightily pleased, better than I ever expected, with the history and the shows of it.'

There were at least twelve revivals in the eighteenth century. In 1727 was the famous one at Drury Lane, at which the management spent £1000 on the coronation scene alone. Most of the great actors and actresses are associated with it, and theatrical anecdote concerning the business used by them is still current. When Colley Cibber declaimed the lines

This candle burns not clear; 'tis I must snuff it;
Then out it goes . . . (III. ii. 97)

he imitated snuffing a candle with a pair of snuffers!

The same popularity continued in the nineteenth century; Kemble, Kean and Macready starred in it, and Mrs. Siddons made a traditionally great Queen Katharine. In more recent times Irving gave a great production of it in 1892 at the Lyceum; he himself played Wolsey; Ellen Terry, Katharine; and Forbes Robertson, Buckingham. And it was *Henry VIII* that Beerbohm Tree brought to New York to celebrate Shakespeare's tercentenary in 1916, a choice that must have made Shakespeare turn in his grave! This production, also, stressed the scenic values of the play, more than the acting.

Appendix C

Authorship of the Play

The question of the authorship of *Henry VIII* is still partly unsolved. It is assigned to Shakespeare chiefly because it appears in the First Folio of 1623. That was edited by Heminges and Condell, two actors who had been in Shakespeare's company and who, by contemporary reports, had had parts in this particular play. The assumption is that when it is classed by them among Shakespeare's plays, they knew what they were talking about. On the other hand, it has been pointed out that the publication of the First Folio was a commercial venture, involving separate copyrights, and that, while the play, *Henry VIII*, was undoubtedly played by Shakespeare's company, it does not necessarily follow that he wrote the whole of it, the major part of it, or even any of it at all. As early as 1758 it was remarked that certain parts of the play have metrical peculiarities unlike Shakespeare's style. But it was not until a hundred years later that James Spedding, led by a remark of the poet Tennyson, made a careful investigation, and published his results in the *Gentleman's Magazine*, in 1850. Aside from subtler criteria, the great test is the proportionately large use of the eleven syllable line, the so-called feminine ending. As an example chosen at random, take the Chamberlain's speech in I. iii. The extra syllables are italicized.

'As far as I can see, all the good our En*glish*
Have got by the late voyage is but mere*ly*
A fit or two o' the face; but they are shrewd *ones;*
For when they hold 'em, you would swear direct*ly*
Their very noses had been counsellors
To Pepin or Clotharius, they keep state *so*.'

It is easy to rewrite this without many such endings.

'As far as I can see, all the good our English
Have got by the late voyage is but slight,
A fit or two o' the face; but they are shrewd;
For when they hold 'em, you would swear at once
Their very noses had been counsellors
To Pepin or Clotharius, they so keep state.'

It is not the question whether one type of verse is better than the other,—in the passage selected, neither is particularly good,—the point is that whereas Shakespeare in his known works uses this extra syllable comparatively rarely, such frequent use of the extra syllable is the characteristic of the style of Shakespeare's great contemporary dramatist, John Fletcher. The reader can amuse himself by testing the lines. Spedding drew up the following table:

Act	Scene	Lines	Red. Syll.	Proportion	Author
1	1	225	63	1 to 3.5	Shakespeare
	2	215	74	1 to 2.9	Shakespeare
	3 & 4	172	100	1 to 1.7	Fletcher
2	1	164	97	1 to 1.6	Fletcher
	2	129	77	1 to 1.6	Fletcher
	3	107	41	1 to 2.6	Shakespeare
	4	230	72	1 to 3.1	Shakespeare
3	1	166	119	1 to 1.3	Fletcher
	2 (to King's exit)	193	62	1 to 3	Shakespeare
	3	257	152	1 to 1.6	Fletcher
4	1	116	57	1 to 2	Fletcher
	2	80	51	1 to 1.5	Fletcher
	3	93	51	1 to 1.8	Fletcher
5	1	176	68	1 to 2.5	Shakespeare (altered)
	2	217	115	1 to 1.8	Fletcher
	3	almost all prose			Fletcher
	4	73	44	1 to 1.6	Fletcher

To account for the conditions as shown in the table above there are only three possible explanations. (1) Shakespeare wrote the whole play but for some unaccountable reason in many of the scenes imitated the style of Fletcher. This is the explanation given by Sir Sidney Lee. (2) Shakespeare and Fletcher collaborated. Collaboration between two or more playwrights was very common in the Elizabethan age. But here almost every great scene is written by Fletcher. If *Henry VIII* was a 'new' play in 1613, Shakespeare had already written *Macbeth, Hamlet,* and *Lear;* he was a veteran dramatist with an established reputation. The question consequently arises why under these circumstances the younger writer should take all the great opportunities and the older do merely the filling in. (3) Shakespeare had no hand in the play whatever; it was merely played under his direction. The non-Fletcherian scenes are not by Shakespeare, but by Massinger. This explanation was suggested in the eighties of the last century by Mr. Robert Boyle. It has recently been argued by Mr. H. Dugdale Sykes, largely on the ground of coincidences of phrasing between *Henry VIII* and Massinger's known plays. It may be interesting to compare the table made by Mr. Sykes with the table of Spedding.

Prologue	Fletcher
Act 1, Sc. 1	Massinger
2	Massinger
3	Massinger & Fletcher
4	Massinger & Fletcher
Act 2, Sc. 1	Massinger & Fletcher
2	Fletcher
3	Massinger
4	Massinger
Act 3, Sc. 1	Massinger & Fletcher
2 (to exit of King)	Massinger
(from exit of King)	Fletcher
Act 4, Sc. 1	Massinger
2	Massinger & Fletcher
Act 5, Sc. 1	Massinger
2	Fletcher
3	Massinger & Fletcher

4	Fletcher
5	Fletcher
Epilogue	Massinger

As a possible explanation of the peculiarities of the play and its passing under Shakespeare's name, Mr. Leicester Bradner suggests that Shakespeare's company suddenly required a play on the general subject of Henry VIII to balance the successful performance of Rowley's *When You See Me, You Know Me* at a rival theatre. This is, of course, only guesswork.

In conclusion: The play was hastily thrown together. It shows no one creative mind. It is a series of scenes, taken from well-known books, scenes which have little relation, even chronological, between them. It has no development of character. And its versification is, in the main, non-Shakespearean. Therefore the conclusion seems inevitable that whatever Shakespeare's share may have been in its composition, it was the minimum amount necessary to have it included by his first editors among his works.

Appendix D

The Text of the Present Edition

The text of the present volume is based, by permission of the Oxford University Press, upon that of the Oxford Shakespeare, edited by the late W. J. Craig. Craig's text has been carefully collated with the Shakespeare Folio of 1623, and the following deviations have been introduced:

1. The stage directions of the Folio have been restored. Necessary words and directions, omitted by the Folio, are added within square brackets.

2. Spelling has been normalized to accord with modern English practice; e.g., Blackfriars, Sandys, everywhere, warlike, vainglory, reverend, sovereign (instead of Black-Friars, Sands, every where, warlike, vain-glory, rev'rend, sov'reign). The punctuation has been largely revised, and a number of old-fashioned Folio forms restored; e.g., th' effects, t' aspire, y' are (you're), burthen (burden).

3. The following changes of text have been introduced, usually in accordance with Folio authority. The readings of the present edition precede the colon, while Craig's readings follow it.

I. i. 42-45 All was royal . . . his full function (assigned to Buckingham F): (assigned to Norfolk)
    47 As you guess (assigned to Norfolk F): (assigned to Buck.)
    63 a' (O F): he
    78 upon,—: upon;
    80 in,—: in
   120 venom'd-mouth'd F: venom-mouth'd
   144 till 't F: till it
 ii. 32 longing F: 'longing
    57 compels F: compel
 147, 148 Henton F: Hopkins

160   *The Life of King Henry the Eighth*

	190	Bulmer: Blumer F
iii.	59	h'as (Ha's F): he has
iv.	77	'em F: them
	86	Ye F: You
II. i.	53	S. d. (Follows line 54 in Craig)
	106	'em F: them
ii.	7	'em F: them
	60	has (ha's F): hath
	64	Who's F: Who is
	99	mine F: my
	107	unpartial F: impartial
iii.	97	moe (mo F): more
iv.	125	Gent. Ush. F: Grif.
	183	many-maz'd: many maz'd F
	215	I then F: Then I
	223	drives F: drive
III. i.	65	in a F: in
	114, 115	you F: ye
	118	h'as (ha's F): he has
	157	'em F: them
ii.	30	letters F: letter
	32	How that F: That
	78	in's F: in his
	103	An F: A
	234	lords F: lord
	400	him F: 'em
	443	by it F: by 't
IV. i.	79	before 'em F: before them
ii.	49	an humble F: a humble
	50	honour. From F: honour from
V. i.	11	and F: an
	172, 173	an F: a
iii.	73	y' are F: you are
	107	Chan.: Cham. F
	133	his F: this
	177	he's F: he is
iv.	2	Parish-garden (Parish Garden F): **Paris-garden**
	7	ye F: you
	86	y' are F: ye 're
v.	76	H'as ('Has F): He has

Appendix E

Suggestions for Collateral Reading

W. G. Boswell-Stone: *Shakespere's Holinshed.* London, 1896. Here the passages of the play are compared with those from the *Chronicle*.

George Cavendish: *The Life of Cardinal Wolsey.* The New Universal Library, with an introduction by Henry Morley. This account of Wolsey by one who knew him well is accessible in a number of editions.

J. S. Brewer: *The Reign of Henry VIII, from his Accession to the Death of Wolsey.* London, 1884. This is the most detailed history of the period. Brewer's admiration for Wolsey's statesmanship blinds him to faults in his character.

J. A. Froude: *The Reign of Henry VIII.* Everyman's Library. Froude's bias against Wolsey will correct Brewer's bias for him.

Martin Hume: *The Wives of Henry VIII.* London, 1905. Katharine's character and her place in history.

James Spedding: *Who Wrote Shakespeare's Henry VIII? Gentleman's Magazine,* August, 1850. The famous discussion of the appearance of Fletcher's style in the play.

Robert Boyle: *Henry VIII.* New Shakespeare Society, 1880, 1886. Massinger's authorship is here upheld.

H. Dugdale Sykes: *Sidelights on Shakespeare.* Stratford-on-Avon, 1919. Massinger's authorship argued on the ground of analogous phrasing between his known plays and *Henry VIII*.

Baldwin Maxwell: *Fletcher and Henry the Eighth.* Manly Memorial Vol., 1923, pp. 104-112. Some doubts concerning Fletcher's alleged part in the play.

Almost any modern edition will discuss the problems involved. The Cambridge edition of *Henry VIII*, edited by Aldus Wright, and the Arden edition, edited by D. Nichol Smith, give large amounts of illustrative material.

INDEX OF WORDS GLOSSED

(Figures in full-faced type refer to page-numbers)

a': **4** (I. i. 63)
abhor: **50** (II. iv. 79)
abject object: **7** (I. i. 127)
advertise: **54** (II. iv. 176)
allay: **35** (II. i. 152)
allegiant: **71** (III. ii. 177)
allow'd: **15** (I. ii. 83)
an: **78** (III. ii. 376)
angels' faces: **62** (III. i. 144)
an't: **57** (III. i. 16)
appliance: **7** (I. i. 124)
apt: **52** (II. iv. 120)
as: **57** (III. i. 7)
avaunt, the: **42** (II. iii. 10)
avoid: **98** (V. i. 85)

baiting: **114** (V. iv. 87)
beaten . . . out of play: **22** (I. iii. 44, 45)
beholding: **25** (I. iv. 41)
Bevis: **3** (I. i. 38)
blister'd: **22** (I. iii. 31)
bombards: **114** (V. iv. 87)
book: **7** (I. i. 122)
bores: **7** (I. i. 128)
bound: **16** (I. ii. 112)
bow'd, three-pence: **43** (II. iii. 36)
brazier: **112** (V. iv. 43)
broken with: **96** (V. i. 47)
by: **49** (II. iv. 47)

camlet: **114** (V. iv. 95)
capable of our flesh: **104** (V. iii. 11, 12)
carriage: **62** (III. i. 160)
carry it so: **16** (I. ii. 134)
challenge: **50** (II. iv. 75)
chambers: **26** (I. iv. 49 S. d.)
changes: **90** (IV. ii. 82 S. d.)

cheveril: **43** (II. iii. 32)
chine: **112** (V. iv. 27)
chronicles of my doing: **15** (I. ii. 74)
clinquant: **3** (I. i. 19)
Clotharius: **21** (I. iii. 10)
clubs: **113** (V. iv. 54)
Colbrand: **112** (V. iv. 23)
collars of esses: **83** (IV. i. 36 S. d.)
colour: **9** (I. i. 178)
colt's tooth: **22** (I. iii. 48)
combination: **9** (I. i. 169)
commends: **44** (II. iii. 61)
compell'd fortune: **45** (II. iii. 87)
comptrollers: **23** (I. iii. 67)
conceit: **45** (II. iii. 74)
conclave, holy: **40** (II. ii. 100)
confederacy: **12** (I. ii. 3)
confirmation: **110** (V. iii. 173)
congee: **90** (IV. ii. 82 S. d.)
contrary: **64** (III. ii. 26); **71** (III. ii. 183)
contrary, on the: **29** (II. i. 15)
convented: **96** (V. i. 52)
cope: **15** (I. ii. 78)
count-cardinal: **9** (I. i. 172)
covent: **88** (IV. ii. 19)
cow, for a: **112** (V. iv. 28)
cross: **72** (III. ii. 215)
cum privilegio: **22** (I. iii. 34)
cure: **25** (I. iv. 33)
current music: **22** (I. iii. 47)

dare: **75** (III. ii. 283)
deriv'd: **48** (II. iv. 30)

device and practice: **10** (I. i. 204)
digest: **66** (III. ii. 53)
discovers: **106** (V. iii. 71)
dispos'd: **16** (I. ii. 116)

emballing: **44** (II. iii. 47)
envious: **30** (II. i. 45)
envy: **61** (III. i. 112)
equal: **40** (II. ii. 108)
estate: **38** (II. ii. 70); **97** (V. i. 74)
evils: **32** (II. i. 67)
example: **15** (I. ii. 90)
exclamation: **14** (I. ii. 52)
exhalation: **73** (III. ii. 227)

fail, upon our: **17** (I. ii. 145)
faints me, it: **46** (II. iii. 103)
fashion: **94** (IV. ii. 160)
fetch in: **5** (I. i. 80)
fierce: **4** (I. i. 54)
fil'd: **70** (III. ii. 172)
file: **13** (I. ii. 42)
fire-drake: **112** (V. iv. 46)
fit o' the face: **20** (I. iii. 7)
flaw'd the league: **6** (I. i. 95)
fool and feather: **21** (I. iii. 25)
force: **63** (III. ii. 2)
fore-skirt: **46** (II. iii. 98)
fortunes, both my: **93** (IV. ii. 142)
front: **13** (I. ii. 42)

gap and trade: **96** (V. i. 36)
Garter: **114** (V. v. S. d.)
gave: **108** (V. iii. 109)
gives way to: **64** (III. ii. 16)
God's dew: **50** (II. iv. 78)
government: **52** (II. iv. 136)
great in admiration: **116** (V. v. 43)
guarded: **1** (Pro. 16)
Guy, Sir: **112** (V. iv. 23)

hair, in her: **83** (IV. i. 36 S. d.)

hand: **75** (III. ii. 300)
hand, made a fine: **113** (V. iv. 76)
happily: **87** (IV. ii. 10); **98** (V. i. 85)
hardly conceive: **16** (I. ii. 105)
h'as: **23** (I. iii. 59)
have-at-him: **39** (II. ii. 85)
having: **43** (II. iii. 23); **70** (III. ii. 160)
head: **33** (II. i. 108)
him in eye: **3** (I. i. 30)
holidame: **99** (V. i. 117)
hulling: **54** (II. iv. 197)

ill husband: **69** (III. ii. 143)
in: **51** (II. iv. 101)
incens'd: **96** (V. i. 43)
Indian, strange: **112** (V. iv. 35)
indifferent: **48** (II. iv. 15)
indurance: **99** (V. i. 122)
instant: **11** (I. i. 225)
intend: **1** (Pro. 21)
issue: **15** (I. ii. 90)
issues: **75** (III. ii. 292)
item: **76** (III. ii. 321)
its: **3** (I. i. 18)

jaded: **74** (III. ii. 281)

keech: **4** (I. i. 55)
knock it: **23** (I. iv. 108)

larder: **111** (V. iv. 5)
late: **95** (V. i. 13)
leave: **91** (IV. ii. 94)
letters-patents: **73** (III. ii. 251)
level: **12** (I. ii. 2)
like: **6** (I. i. 100)
Limbo Patrum: **113** (V. iv. 69)
line, under the: **112** (V. iv. 45)

King Henry the Eighth

little England: **44** (II. iii. 46)
lo you: **10** (I. i. 202)
longing: **13** (I. ii. 32)
loose: **34** (II. i. 127)
lop: **15** (I. ii. 96)
lose: **31** (II. i. 57)
Lucifer: **78** (III. ii. 371)

main: **72** (III. ii. 216)
make my play: **25** (I. iv. 46)
manage: **105** (V. iii. 24)
many-maz'd: **54** (II. iv. 183)
Marshalsea: **114** (V. iv. 92)
mate: **74** (III. ii. 275)
mean: **109** (V. iii. 146)
measure: **28** (I. iv. 106)
mere: **76** (III. ii. 330)
minister communication: **5** (I. i. 86)
mistaken: **10** (I. i. 195)
model: **93** (IV. ii. 133)
modest: **106** (V. iii. 69)
moe: **46** (II. iii. 97)
moiety: **12** (I. ii. 12)
Moorfields: **112** (V. iv. 34)
mortar-piece: **112** (V. iv. 49)
motions: **8** (I. i. 153)
motley coat: **1** (Pro. 16)
mud in Egypt: **46** (II. iii. 92)
music: **91** (IV. ii. 94)

nothing: **99** (V. i. 126)

objections: **76** (III. ii. 308)
of: **109** (V. iii. 136)
open, in: **79** (III. ii. 405)
opinion: **1** (Pro. 20)
opposing: **85** (IV. i. 67)
out of: **64** (III. ii. 13)
out-speaks: **69** (III. ii. 128)

pales: **114** (V. iv. 96)
panging: **42** (II. iii. 15)
papers: **5** (I. i. 80)

paragon'd: **56** (II. iv. 228)
par'd my present havings: **70** (III. ii. 160)
Parish-garden: **111** (V. iv. 2)
part of: **57** (III. i. 24)
parted: **103** (V. ii. 27)
Paul's: **111** (V. iv. 17)
pay the act of it: **71** (III. ii. 183)
Pepin: **21** (I. iii. 10)
period: **20** (I. ii. 209)
perk'd up: **43** (II. iii. 21)
perniciously: **31** (II. i. 50)
person: **53** (II. iv. 153)
pick: **114** (V. iv. 96)
pinked: **112** (V. iv. 51)
pitch: **37** (II. ii. 50)
plainsong: **22** (I. iii. 45)
pleasant: **28** (I. iv. 90)
pluck off: **43** (II. iii. 40)
porringer: **112** (V. iv. 51)
post with packets: **103** (V. ii. 31)
potent circumstances: **50** (II. iv. 74)
powers: **51** (II. iv. 111)
practices: **17** (I. ii. 127); **100** (V. i. 129)
præmunire: **77** (III. ii. 341)
presence: **57** (III. i. 17)
presence, i' the: **88** (IV. ii. 37)
presently: **18** (I. ii. 157)
primero: **95** (V. i. 7)
privity: **5** (I. i. 74)
prodigal: **115** (V. v. 13)
proportion: **100** (V. i. 130)
pursuivants: **103** (V. ii. 23)

quarrel: **42** (II. iii. 14)

rankness: **85** (IV. i. 59)
repeat your will: **12** (I. ii. 13)
return'd in his opinions: **66** (III. ii. 64)

right: **108** (V. iii. 103)
roads: **88** (IV. ii. 17)
round: **114** (V. iv. 86)
rub: **34** (II. i. 129)
running banquet: **24** (I. iv. 12); **113** (V. iv. 71)

Saba: **116** (V. v. 24)
sacring bell: **75** (III. ii. 296)
sad: **1** (Pro. 3)
salute: **46** (II. iii. 103)
Samson: **112** (V. iv. 23)
saw: **2** (I. i. 2)
sectary: **106** (V. iii. 70)
seeming: **51** (II. iv. 106)
self-drawing web: **4** (I. i. 63)
set, was: **59** (III. i. 73)
several: **29** (II. i. S. d.)
shrewd: **110** (V. iii. 177)
shrouds: **85** (IV. i. 72)
sick: **15** (I. ii. 82)
sign: **51** (II. iv. 106)
silenc'd: **6** (I. i. 97)
simony: **88** (IV. ii. 36)
slightly: **51** (II. iv. 110)
so: **70** (III. ii. 173)
sometimes: **54** (II. iv. 179)
sound: **102** (V. ii. 12)
spare your spoons: **110** (V. iii. 166)
spavin: **21** (I. iii. 12)
speak: **53** (II. iv. 164); **61** (III. i. 124); **88** (IV. ii. 32)
spleen: **18** (I. ii. 174)
spleeny Lutheran: **68** (III. ii. 100)
springhalt: **21** (I. iii. 13)
stand on: **99** (V. i. 123)
state: **1** (Pro. 3); **12** (I. ii. 8 S. d.); **55** (II. iv. 211)
stick them in our will: **15** (I. ii. 94)
stomach: **88** (IV. ii. 34)
stood to: **50** (II. iv. 84)
Strand: **113** (V. iv. 56)

sufferance: **42** (II. iii. 15)
suggestion: **88** (IV. ii. 35)
suggests: **9** (I. i. 164)
suit of pounds: **45** (II. iii. 85)
suns of glory: **2** (I. i. 6)

take you out: **28** (I. iv. 95)
talker: **39** (II. ii. 79)
tall stockings: **21** (I. iii. 30)
temperance: **7** (I. i. 124)
tender: **51** (II. iv. 114)
that: **3** (I. i. 38); **118** (Epil. 7)
top-proud: **8** (I. i. 151)
touch: **53** (II. iv. 153); **95** (V. i. 13)
trace: **65** (III. ii. 45)
tract: **4** (I. i. 40)
trembling: **15** (I. ii. 95)

understand: **22** (I. iii. 32)
unhappily: **28** (I. iv. 89)
unpartial: **40** (II. ii. 107)
unthink your speakng: **51** (II. iv. 102)
us'd: **63** (III. i. 175)

venom'd: **7** (I. i. 120)
vouch: **8** (I. i. 157)
vouchsafe: **44** (II. iii. 43)

way: **95** (V. i. 28)
ween: **100** (V. i. 136)
weigh: **99** (V. i. 125)
weigh out: **60** (III. i. 87)
well said: **25** (I. iv. 30)
wife, way I am: **58** (III. i. 38)
will: **15** (I. ii. 94)
withal: **69** (III. ii. 131)
work: **113** (V. iv. 63)
working: **1** (Pro. 3)
worship: **4** (I. i. 39)
wrought: **76** (III. ii. 312)

York-place: **86** (IV. i. 94)